THE THREE TREES

— ※ —

Notes from my Journals

CURT ILES

Contents

The Three Trees		1
1. Prologue: Relationships		5
2. Three Trees: Three Stories		9
3. Just Show Up		13
4. Journaling		16
5. Humility		21
6. Generosity		25
7. The Happiest Sled Dog		31
8. A Loser's Limp		36
9. Sail On		39
10. Lifting the Barn		43
11. L.L.L. Lifelong Learning		47
12. Be a Reader		53
13. If You Like People		59
14. The 10-4-2 Rule		62
15. Active Listening		79
16. The Sweetest Sound		81
17. The Power of a Hand-Written Note		83

18.	Friend-Keeping	87
19.	Grit	94
20.	Dream Stealers and Joy Killers	101
21.	Coasting	108
22.	Ruts	112
23.	The Ministry of Presence	115
24.	High Expectations	122
25.	A Woman Named Lou	124
26.	Choose Your Hill Carefully	128
27.	Finding Your Jethro	137
28.	Gratitude	144
29.	How's Your Walk?	148
30.	Take a Knee	151
31.	The Empty Chair	159
32.	In the Word	162
33.	Receiving and Giving Gifts	169
34.	Integrity: Doing the Right Thing	174
35.	Kindness	181
36.	Encouragement	186
37.	Stewardship	190
38.	The 30,000 Foot View	198
39.	A Life Plan	207
40.	Circles	221
41.	Buckets	226

42.	Beware of Leaky Buckets	230
43.	Why I Write . . . And Why You Should, Too	233
44.	Burned yet Blessed	242
45.	Keep Your Feet on the Ground	248
46.	A Vista with "Noodle" and "Pilgrim"	253
47.	Finishing Strong	256
48.	Epilogue: A Log Older Than Louisiana	261
49.	End Notes	267
50.	The Tree	278

THE THREE TREES

Notes from my Journals

CURT ILES

With Noah Iles

DEDICATION

To my precious Aunt JoAnn Iles Edwards who has always seen the best in me. Aunt Jo, I dedicate this book to you in honor of your passion to keep our rich family roots deep and strong.

"The best time to plant a tree is twenty years ago. The next best time is today."

CURT ILES

Also by Curt Iles

Stories from the Creekbank

The Old House

Wind in the Pines

Hearts Across the Water

Deep Roots

The Mockingbird's Midnight Song

Christmas Jelly

The Wayfaring Stranger

A Good Place

As the Crow Flies

A Spent Bullet

Trampled Grass

Uncle Sam: A Horse's Tale

Where I Come From

THE THREE TREES

All books are available on Amazon/Ingram in paperback, hardcover, ebook, and large print formats.

Author page: www.amazon.com/author/creekbank.stories

Website: www.creekbank.net

Email: creekbank.stories@gmail.com

Facebook: @TheCreekTribe

Cover design by Matheus Alves, Ugly Mug Marketing, Alexandria, Louisiana

Sketches by Tim Conner, Vinton, Louisiana

Interior design by Noah Iles

Copyright © 2025 Curt Iles and Creekbank Stories

All rights reserved by Curt Iles and Creekbank Stories. No part of this publication may be reproduced or transmitted in any form without prior permission in writing from the publisher.

The Three Trees: Notes from my Journals

CURT ILES

Library of Congress Number (LOCN) 2025908261

Paperback ISBN   978-0-9863026-7-1

Hardcover ISBN   978-0-9863026-8-8

Ebook   ISBN   978-1-967796-02-1

Large Print ISBN   978-1-967796-03-8

Available from Amazon, Ingram, and other distributors

Creekbank Stories
Curt Iles
Every Journey has a Story.

"Sharing moving stories that encourage and inspire readers."

1

PROLOGUE: RELATIONSHIPS

THE THREE TREES

Notes from my Journals

"When it comes down to it, only two things matter:"
Relationships and Memories."
—Kirk Cooper

I originally wrote this book for my two oldest grandsons. Noah Iles and Jack Iles. Both are both high school seniors stepping out into real life this year. One grandson is going to Louisiana Tech, and the other to the Naval Academy.

I want to share some life wisdom before my influence fades.

I wanted to tell them some stories.

Because that is who I am. I'm a storyteller.

But at some point, *The Three Trees* wrested control from me, took over personal ownership, and decided to tell its own stories in its own way.

I watched, spellbound, as *The Three Trees* became its own book. This book was no longer mine.

I still haven't got the original deed back.

It even went through various name changes than the one you hold in your hands.

Next, it evolved from a book to *two* young men to one essential for *any* youth leaving home, regardless of gender, background, or cultures.

To my astonishment, it kept morphing. *The Three Trees* became a guide for young leaders, then decided it would appeal to leaders of all ages and levels.

It seemed to say, "Good leadership is always about leaders who have a solid common foundation written into their DNA. They have developed a culture around a clear vision for the future and its concepts can serve as a good guidebook."

Finally, *The Three Trees* became the type of book I love.

A book that anyone could enjoy and learn from. It became a book filled with stories of personal growth, perseverance, good Southern manners, and pure old common sense, which is uncommon.

I'm pretty satisfied with the results, even though I didn't really write it.

Let me be clear: I'm not talking about A.I.

Artificial Intelligence will never be able to put into words the true culture and memorable people of the Louisiana Pineywoods.

So, I feel good about my job security. No machine is going to take my place.

So, who actually wrote *The Three Trees*?

It is a heart-book written from the deep in the souls and memories of those I know and others who I only knew about. They're passing on their insights that I always called "The Wisdom of the Woods." I'm simply the conduit.

I'm pretty satisfied with the final results.

I hope you, the reader, will also be pleased.

The writing *experts* say that if you try to write for everyone; you write for no one.

They're right. I write for one group, the human condition, who deep down have the same desires, hopes, dreams, tears, joys, and struggles on this long journey called life.

Regardless of where they live and die.

Next, these *experts* of the writing establishment assert that if you try to write about everything, no one will read it.

This book isn't about everything.

It's about one thing. *Relationships.*

One word.

Relationships.

And everyone's life story boils down to relationships, or the lack thereof.

I'd like to add a sister word to relationships: Memories.

Memories come from relationships.

Relationships and Memories.

Those experienced writing gurus have their assumptions, "Don't write for *everyone* and don't try to about everything."

Read *The Three Trees* and make up your own mind. You, my readers, are the only experts that matter.

I look forward to hearing what *you, the reader*, think.

Always remember, it's about always about Relationships and Memories.

"Hold on to those memories like they're heaven passing through."
—"Heaven Passing Through"
Turnpike Troubadours

Onward,
Curt Iles
May 2025
Dry Creek, Louisiana

2

THREE TREES: THREE STORIES

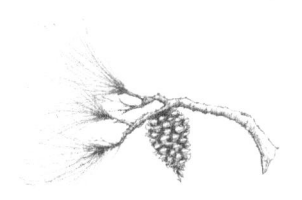

The cover of *The Three Trees* features three trees, each with a unique story.

The small longleaf pine in the foreground has spent most of its young life in a grassy stage with little visible growth. However, it has steadily grown a deep taproot and at some point, when conditions are right, will begin its long skyward journey.

Behind it stands a majestic, mature longleaf pine. This native Louisiana tree can live for over 150 years. It's the Mother Tree and most of the younger pines, which have come from the big pine cones and their seeds.

There's a third tree on the cover. It's the thin skeleton of a dead tree, ready to be toppled by the next storm. This tree has completed its job by dropping years of seeds.

This blackened tree reminds me of my Dry Creek ancestors and mentors who passed on their common sense wisdom. They're gone, but I'm here to pass on what they modeled. It's a deep call that compels me to write, speak, and share.

Each of my mentors had a story to tell.

I listened. I'm now passing them on to you.

I want to speak to those grassy-stage pines. I have some stories that will help them on their journey.

I've come to view life as a succession of seasons.

Each of the three trees are in different seasons.

Growth.

Maturity.

Death.

I'm at that tall, mature longleaf stage. There's plenty of sap in me as well as a deep taproot. I'm in the season where I want to pass on the heritage and culture of the Louisiana Pineywoods which have shaped my life.

The Three Trees contain stories about the values and habits a young person needs as they step into life. These stories transcend age, gender, culture, and background. It's also a valuable guide for leaders of all ages who want to maintain their priorities and follow their moral compass.

That's why I want to share *The Three Trees*. There are many grassy stage pines surrounding me that weren't brought up in my culture.

THE THREE TREES

I want to pass on the rich rural values that the old, blackened trees taught me that have withstood the test of time.

Lessons about the things that really matter.

Finding that purpose for your life journey

I believe I'd found my current purpose in life. It's writing and share moving stories that inspire and encourage.

There is it. I Write. Share Moving Stories. Inspire. Encourage.

May I be a good steward of this assignment with *The Three Trees*.

"The shortest distance between the truth and a human heart is a story."
-Anthony DeMello

Above all, I'm a storyteller.

Remember that this as we start this journey together through the pages of *The Three Trees*,

I'm also a story collector.

I collect them like some people collect Mardi Gras beads.

I truly believe stories have the power to change us.

As DeMello's quote says it all, *Connecting human hearts and the truth.*

That's what a story does.

To change how we look at others as well as ourselves.

My hope and prayer is that as you travel through a lifetime of my journals, you'll find your own life story.

And write it down.

To pass on to those dearest to you.

That's legacy.

Passing it on.

Finally, I hope you will find purpose in each step you make, and hopefully become the best man or woman God made you to be.

So join me as we walk onward and up.

Walking together on my land in Dry Creek, through the longleafs, along Crooked Bayou, before stopping to sit together on the Old House porch.

It'll be a memorable trip.

NOTES TO MY FUTURE SELF:

3

Just Show Up

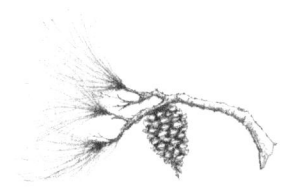

Let's start with something simple. It's something every person can—and—should do.

Just show up.

That's it.

It's a significant measure of success. Just show up every day.

It's incredible what a difference that will make in the arc of your life.

If you're in school, don't sleep in and miss that 7:45 am class.

Students who attend class usually pass. Those who skip class often don't.

Just show up.

You may be in the workforce. Show up every day.

Don't miss unless it's a genuine emergency. If so, phone in at once.

Show up for wherever you're supposed to be.

My friend Mollie Bailey runs Grant Christmas Tree Farm with her husband, Gray. The day after Thanksgiving (Black Friday) is their biggest tree sale day, with thousands attending.

It takes over one hundred workers to make it work.

I'm the early greeter, so I see folks as they arrive. Mollie hustles past me in the early morning light. "Curt, It's *unbelievable* how many calls I received last night informing me they couldn't come to work because a shopping trip or a family event had come up."

I agree. *Unbelievable.*

Man, if you're supposed to be somewhere, show up.

And get there early.

Don't rush in right at time.

I have a friend who says, "If you're not ten minutes early, you're late."

Don't use that snooze button. It's made for losers.

Get out of bed and get your day started.

Get after it.

Just show up. It's a big deal, and it's still a big deal to do the small things, and do them right.

> "But here's the thing . . . People are always looking for the secret shortcut that changes everything, but those are rare. Great success more often comes from doing a lot of little things well: tweaking, fine-tuning."
> —W. Clement Stone

There it is: Just show up and work hard!

NOTES TO MY FUTURE SELF:

4

Journaling

There's no wrong way to keep a journal.

I've written on napkins, backs of envelopes. I once jotted a story outline on T.P.

I use a pencil because I like to erase.

Next, I return with pen, highlighter, and sharpie..

Your instrument can be a cheap Bic pen, stubby pen, or an expensive gift pen.

Choose your weapon of choice. All you need is something to write with.

And something to write in . . . or in.

Live a memorable story and keep a record of it.

Vocalize your life.

Keep memorable notes.

My dad was a land surveyor.
He always carried a small booklet in his front pocket.
He called it his field notes.
Daddy would peer through his transit scope, pull a stubby pencil from behind his ear and scribble notes, sketches, diagrams, and distances.
He used his field book to record things that were important.
Details he'd need to recall later.

Although I didn't grow up to follow his career, I believe I'm more of a surveyor than I realized.
I peer through this fascinating scope called life.
Then I get out my field notes, which I call a journal, and jot down my ideas with a pencil.
I *journal* notes.
I journal. Yes, it's a verb. An action verb.
I *grab* those ideas and *journal* before they can escape and fly off.
I hold them in a death grip until I can jot them down on paper.
Sadly, we let hundreds of great stories fly off without capturing them.
That's why I've filled hundreds of journals since my teenage years.

They are the stories of the ups and downs, joys, and sorrows of my life.

People I've met.

People I've loved.

People I've lost.

For decades before I had any thought of being a public author, I kept field notes.

I wrote in my journal.

What I wrote things I wanted to remember, knowing most of it would never see the light of day.

I was doing what I was called to do.

Like Daddy, I was taking field notes.

I still am.

It was Christmas 1973. I was a seventeen-year-old high school senior.

The present was from my Uncle Bill.

Always my favorite uncle.

He still is.

I held the cheap brown booklet in my hand, then flipped it open. It was a blank journal.

There was a handwritten note encouraging me to write about my life. Here's a portion of what Uncle Bill wrote:

"Write about the things that turn you on—the things you like and the things you love.

Also, write about the pain you see and feel—the things that upset you or disturb you.

In writing these things down in this, your little book, you will discover parts of yourself that lie deep within, next to the soul of your being . . ."

I still have the faded original note, tucked in Journal #1, surrounded on each side by the hundreds of journals I've penned since then.

Most of them will never see the light of day. That's fine. The process of putting my thoughts on paper made me a better man.

Uncle Bill, it's still the best Christmas present I've ever received.

Here is the final excerpt from Uncle Bill's journal advice:

"Just write.

Find your own style.

Write about the things that move you: joy, tears, laughter, grief, life, and death.

But just write."*

"Soft wind blowing in the pines.
"A mockingbird begins to sing.
A woman lullabies her child
As evening spreads her wings.
Let nature sing.
Let nature sing.
A sweet harmony.
A never-ending melody.
Let nature sing."

"Let Nature Sing"
—Dickey Betts
(Copied from a 1970s journal.)

*From the book *Christmas Jelly* by Curt Iles "The Best Christmas Present I Ever Received."

Available on Amazon.

NOTES TO MY FUTURE SELF:

5

Humility

"Your deepest pain can give you the highest platform."

Before you get very far into *The Three Trees* and I share my founts of wisdom, which some friends jokingly call "The World According to Curt Iles."

I laugh with them. I'm not sure if it's a compliment or not.

Let me properly introduce myself.

I'm Curt Iles, and I'm a broken man.

Just like most of you, I've been broken and am a fellow struggler along this journey called life.

Here's my broken story as told by a coffee cup.

When my favorite coffee cup fell onto the patio floor, it shattered, and shards scattered about.

The handle broke off, and a sizeable crescent-shaped piece of the rim was gone. Sadly, it would now only hold three sips of coffee.

I really liked its rough ceramic finish and how it kept my coffee hot, but now it was useless. I walked to the trash can . . . and then stopped.

Instead of tossing the cup, I retrieved a Sharpie and wrote across the bottom, "I've broken, but I'm still useful."

I can understand that because I've been broken, too.

My brokenness comes from periodic bouts of deep depression.

Many times during those dark times, I felt as if I was broken beyond repair. My depression was so deep, dark, and long that I doubted that I'd survive or ever be of use again.

However, I was wrong; In God's economy, nothing is wasted. He takes everything in our lives and shapes us to be more useful for the Kingdom.

So, despite my dark valleys, I'm still useful. The fact that you're reading this book means God can still use broken people.

My depression has made me a better and more empathic man, and it's given me a platform and a voice to encourage others suffering from this illness.

Those of you who've been with me through my previous books will notice a difference in my writing.

I've been broken and put back together again.

That changes everything about a man, including how he sees the world and writes about it.

And my brokenness gave me a healthy dose of humility.

It's hard to be cocky when you've come out of the darkness.

Depression.

Notice the combat terms used in describing depression:

"I'm battling depression. "

"It's a fight."

"He's gone through bouts of depression."

"I've struggled with depression."

These descriptive words have a commonality: depression is a great struggle and a fierce fight that tests everything within a man or woman.

It's a battle.

That describes my depression. I've battled it.

If I can get as low as I was and bounce back—anyone can. I'm the poster child for hope and healing.

You will get better. Don't give up hope.

Hold onto hope. It's a precious commodity.

Grasp that strong rope called hope.

You're not hopeless. God isn't through with you yet.
You will get better. Don't let go of the rope.
Your brokenness will probably differ from mine.
Life has a way of sooner or later breaking all of all of us.
Remember that God makes us stronger in these broken places.
And I repeat: Brokenness teaches us humility.
And that ain't a bad thing.

So, as you read through this book called *The Three Trees*, I hope you can sense this thread of humility in my stories.

I may sound as if I've got it all together, but remember, I'm a fellow struggler along the journey.

What you'll find on the pages of *The Three Trees* are simply dropped crumbs on the trail behind me. I hope those crumbs lead you as you travel.

Crumbs.

Left for you to help along your way.

I'm still learning.

Yes, I've been broken.

And that ain't a bad thing.

NOTES TO MY FUTURE SELF:

6

GENEROSITY

You simply cannot out give God, so be generous in all things.
And generosity involves so much more than finances.
It includes every aspect of our lives: time, love, energy, attention, and a spirit of bigheartedness.

Sadly, the opposite of generosity is hoarding. Holding onto something instead of being willing to share. That's a shame and a sad way to live.

However, we have the choice. We can be a miserly old skinflint or discover the joy of giving.

We have the *privilege* to be generous.

Two of my dearest are friends are Karl and Gene Ortis. You cannot talk very long with Gene without hearing wisdom and stories from his parents, Albert, and Lucille Ortis.

Albert Ortis lived in Krotz Springs along the Atchafalaya River. He was a hard worker, inventor/innovator, a commercial fishermen, built the town's first ice plant, and on the side, built tugboats.

Most of all, he was a committed follower of Jesus.

Albert Ortis was also a generous man who understood about stewardship.

Gene Ortis shared about his father's philosophy of generosity:

You can't love without giving. Extra is what you have received. Extra is what you should give.

Make heavenly investments. There are no trailer hitches on hearses. If you are going to invest in heaven, you have to do it here and now.

If we send our investments on ahead, then our actions will be weaned from the perishable things of this world. Generosity pleases God.

Heavenly investments are fully insured.

It all belongs to God. We are caretakers, not permanent owners. All property will one day revert to its original owner.

Gene said, "Dad believed and lived these things until his dying breath."

I feel poorer for not having met Alberta and Lucille Ortis. However, their lives are still speaking through their kind deeds and this story.

"Don't say anything you wouldn't want to see flying behind an airplane."
—Lucille Ortis

It truly is more blessed to give than to receive.

The basketball across the street bounced about fourteen hours a day during the summer. Our neighbors had a dilapidated basketball goal with a broken plastic backboard and a bent rim.

But that didn't keep the boys from playing. A group of about six played day and night.

Nothing stopped them. They'd play through rain. In cold weather, they'd be stripped down to T-shirts and shorts.

They had a dim streetlight, but it shed only shadows on the court.

They kept a constant patter going at all times of day and night. Their games featured hollering and what my generation called *talking jive*.

DeDe and I often went to bed with the thumping and yelling. Many times, they'd be playing as we turned out the lights. We turned the AV unit up and turned my trusty box fan to high.

Although the teams changed daily, a nucleus of about four boys played daily.

There was Kameron and his younger brother, Marcus. The other players went by street names. I'd walk over to speak to them, I knew I was on their turf.

An old-bald—headed-white man didn't fit in on their side of Lark Lane.

They were polite but always cool.

I became determined to break the impasse that stretched across our street.

Just before Christmas I watched out our front window as a spirited game was going full tilt.

That's when I came up with a plan.

I walked across the street, "Hey, Guys. I have some stuff to load and need

need you to go with me."

The ball bounced away as they eyed me suspiciously.

Kameron, the oldest brother said, "We can't go with De'Varius."

Kameron, De'Varius, and three more guys crowded into the truck.

"Where are we going?"

"I need you to help load something heavy."

The rest of the drive was quiet except for low whispering in the back

When I turned into the Academy Sports Store, their ears pricked and they leaned forward.

"What are we doing?"

"Guys, we're going to buy you a new basketball goal.

Kameron hollered and clapped.

Marcus said, "You wouldn't do this for us!"

"Yep, it's your Christmas present from Mrs. DeDe and me."

I'd been blessed recently with excellent book sales and wanted to invest some of it. I'd chosen to invest in these guys.

They picked out a back board and pole. We loaded our gear into the truck. I'd never seen young men boys so excited.

I more fully understood the words of Jesus, "It is more blessed to give than receive."

I'm not sure who enjoyed this gift the most: them or me.

The next morning the old goal was still there and there was no sign of the new one.

I was surprised and walked over. Kameron met and pointed to the garage. All of the parts and hardware were neatly arranged. "We're waiting for Daddy to get home on Christmas Eve. He's on a long haul somewhere up the East Coast."

They erected the goal on Christmas Day, and there's been a running game going day and night.

The bouncing of the ball and yelling doesn't bother me in the least. It sounds like the rhythm of youth and the enjoyment of life.

Of course, I've gone from "old-bald-headed-white-man" to "Big Man on Campus."

Now, when I arrive home from work, they stop their game and wave.

Kameron will often walk slowly across Lark where we'll meet in the middle of the street where he greets me with a firm handshake. The look in his eyes would be worth one hundred new goals.

There we are. The happiest two men on the corner of Lark and Highpoint.

He's happy to have a new basketball goal.

And I'm equally happy to have given it.

Sounds like a fair trade to me.

Be generous.

The generous life is the best life to live.

"Remember the words of our Lord, "It is more blessed to give than receive." —The Apostle Paul quoting Jesus in Acts 20:35.

I'd never argue with either of those two.
It truly is a privilege to give.
To give.
Be generous.
You'll never regret living the generous life.

"You Get What You Give"

"Don't let go, you've got the music in you.
One dance left, this world is gonna pull through
Don't give up, you've got a reason to live
Can't forget, *we only get what we give*
Don't let go, I feel the music in you."

—"You Get What You Give"
The New Radicals

NOTES TO MY FUTURE SELF:

7

THE HAPPIEST SLED DOG

A sled dog is happiest when he's in the traces.

It's true about sled dogs. They're happiest when they're working hard and pulling together.

Work is good for us.

We all have this distorted view that work is the punishment of original sin. Adam and Eve sinned, left the garden, and God consigned them to a prison sentence of work.

Yet, the Scriptures make it clear Adam and Eve had work *before* the Fall:

The Lord God took the man and put him in the Garden of Eden to work it and take care of it. (Genesis 2:15)

It's only after the first couple sinned that the briars and birth pangs began.

Mankind's first job was "to *work* it and *take care* of the land."

God blessed them and said to them, "Be fruitful and increase in number; fill the earth and subdue it." (Genesis 1.28)

God even gave Adam a job description:

Be fruitful

Increase in number

Fill the earth

Subdue it

Each term involves work of some kind.

We're meant to be doers, not sitters.

Plowers of the field, not spectators.

It's a shame how many people dread work as a four-letter word.

Having a job and purpose is one of life's joys. Like the sled dog, we're wired to work.

One of my favorite Jason Isbell songs is "Something to Love." It's written to his daughter, and has this memorable line:

"I hope you find something to love
Something to do when you feel like giving up
A song to sing or a tale to tell
Something to love, it'll serve you well."

I don't think my father ever enjoyed his job. Daddy never explained this to me. He wasn't one to talk about something that deep.

He worked for thirty years with the Highway Department as a road surveyor. He was good at his job. His co-workers admired and respected Daddy and he got along with everyone very well.

Surveying was his job, but it was never his calling.

He had a job and a calling.

But they weren't the same.

It saddened me as a teenager to realize that his job didn't fulfill him.

Despite that, Clayton Iles had a calling.

A high calling that never waned.

He was called to work with young people.

He never had a paid youth worker job, but at every stage of his life, he worked with teens.

He loved them, and they loved him in return.

And until he died, he was active in the lives of young people, serving as a spiritual mentor, teacher, and friend. He introduced many of them to a personal relationship with Jesus.

I know that for sure because I was one of those lucky few that got to spend loads of time with him.

Daddy retired from his highway job.

But he remained true to his calling.

You can leave jobs, but you'll never leave your calling.

I'm on my fifth career and I believe in my heart that every change was in the center of God's will. I've never retired and have no plans to.

My calling has been clear since I turned twenty to work with young men and spread encouragement.

I'm still trying. My calling has led to full-time writing and sharing it with others.

I'm still an encourager.

To pour my life into my grandchildren's buckets.

To help the downtrodden as Jesus commanded us to look after "'The least of these.'

Those are facets of my callings

You don't retire from a calling.

It's usually a lifetime passion that follows a man or woman to the deathbed.

The man or woman who can work at his calling is double blessed.

I have a calling.

To write.

I believe it's my assignment for the remaining seasons of my life.

I want to do it well and touch my world, regardless of where it may reach.

I'm often asked,

"Well, how do you like being retired?"

I never quite know how to answer that question. I've never worked harder in my life.

And I've felt more fulfilled and useful.

The following conversations actually occurred:

Standing in line, a lady asked, "Well, what do you do for a living?"

"I'm a *writer*."

She smiled. "Oh, we like *horses*, too."

I should have learned from that encounter when a man later asked, "And now *what* is it you do?"

I hesitated. "Well, I'm a writer."

He slapped my back. "Great. What size bike do you ride?"

I've changed my reply,

"I'm an *author who writes books*."

I know that sounds redundant, but I don't want to be asked again about my horse or my Harley.

Each of must find that something to love.

It may not follow the family business.

It's a very personal journey finding something to love,

Listen to Jason Isbell's final verse to his daughter:

"We turned you loose and tried to stay out of your way

Don't quite recognize the world you call home

Just find what makes you happy girl and do it 'til you're gone."

Yes, find what makes you happy, and do it 'til you're gone.

Sounds like good advice to me.

NOTES TO MY FUTURE SELF:

8

A Loser's Limp

You've seen them.

People with a "Loser's Limp."

What is a loser's limp?

I first read about the loser's limp in *See You at the Top*, a classic book by Zig Ziglar:

"You know what the Loser's Limp is if you've ever attended a football game. The receiver slips past the defensive back, pulls in a pass, and heads for the end zone.

The defensive man quickly recovers and takes out in hot pursuit. When the receiver gets about twenty yards from the end zone, the defensive back realizes he will not catch up with the receiver.

So, the defensive player frequently pulls up limping.

The people in the stands shake their heads and say, "Well, no wonder the poor guy couldn't catch him. Look, he's hurt.'
"Now that is his Loser's Limp. What is yours?"

*See You at the Top by Zig Ziglar
Pelican Press. Available on Amazon

It's so easy to make excuses.

This type of person tries to place the blame somewhere. The weather. A difficult circumstance. A conspiracy. An obstructing boss. A difficult spouse.

They will not take ownership.

It's always easier to blame someone or something else.

I learned so much in Africa, carefully observing the traditions and cultures of each tribe I worked among.

There was a common reaction when something was spilled or broken that always intrigued me.

When someone bumped a coffee cup off a table, shattering it, the offender would point accusingly point at the shattered cup. "That coffee of coffee? It fell off the table."

He was half-right. It fell off the table after he'd knocked it off with a careless elbow,

But it was still, "It just fell off the table . . . "

Don't laugh too loud: Africans don't have copyright on transferring blame.

It exists everywhere. Especially here in the Good Ol' U.S. of A.

My friend, Warren Morris, shares about Coach Skip Bertman's favorite acronym: T.O.B. "Transfer of Blame."

T.O.B. Transfer of Blame. It's human nature to want to blame someone else.

"The weather was too bad."

"The sun was in my eyes."

"It was low and outside, but the ump called it a strike."

"Those refs at Plainview will always cheat you."

"The ball hit a rock."

The all-time lowest T.O.B. "But you made me hit you."

It goes back to the Garden, but that doesn't make it right:

"That *woman* you *gave* me."

T.O.B. in its original sin mode.

We must work hard to eliminate loser limps. whining, and transfer-of-blame from our lives.

Like all ingrained habits, it's hard to eradicate. The first step is giving it a name and recognizing it in ourselves.

Breaking away from always blaming someone or something else.

Taking responsibility is a habit, just like blaming.

Today is National T.O.B. Day.

But isn't every day?

NOTES TO MY FUTURE SELF:

9

SAIL ON

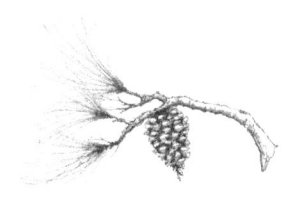

"The safest place for a ship is in the harbor, but ships are not made for that purpose."

Go for it, Man!
Attempt to live a regret free life.
Don't be timid.

The biography of one of my World War II heroes, Admiral Chester Nimitz, states,

"Twenty years earlier in 1922, Chester Nimitz, a student at the Naval War College, had written his thesis on naval tactics. In it, he argued that "Great results cannot be accomplished without a corresponding degree of risk.

"The leader who awaits perfection of plans, material, or training will wait in vain.

And in the end will yield the victory to him who employs the tools at hand with the greatest vigor."

In the last week of May 1942, Nimitz staked everything on an unequal contest with the enemy's main battle fleet. Nimitz's ships attacked the larger Japanese fleet at Midway.

While the Americans lost one carrier in the naval battle, the Japanese lost all of four of their aircraft carriers.

Midway was the decisive naval battle of the Pacific.

Only six months after Pearl Harbor, Nimitz's audacious plan turned the tide of the war."

In spite of the odds, he sent his fleet.
He weighed the risks yet still sailed on.
He sailed out.
He sailed on.

There are many terms for sailing out and going for it.

The Irish call it, "Throwing your hat over the wall."
You must move forward.
Cortez burned his ships on the Mexican coast.
No turning back.
Caesar stood at the tiny Rubicon River with his legions, knowing that crossing the river meant risking war with Rome.

He splashed his horse across the river.

"Come on, Men. Let's go."

He'd crossed the Rubicon.

There was no turning back.

Each of these terms above describes what DeDe and I did in 2012.

We sold our house.

Had a fine estate sale.

I even sold my tractor. I still regret that one.

We left Dry Creek and moved to Africa for three years.

Dry Creek erupted in scandal when we listed our home for sale. The head shaking continued when we sold most of our possessions.

We were in a season where we could follow our dream of going to the mission field.

So we did it.

We jumped.

We sailed out.

It was worth it, although it was never easy.

Often difficult and discouraging.

We were thrust into the fringes of a civil war in South Sudan and worked among thousands of refugees,

But we had a front-row seat at how can God can act in the midst of chaos.

We wouldn't have missed it for the world.

> "It is not because things are difficult that we do not dare; It is because we do not dare that things are difficult."
>
> —Seneca

A final word on the fear of failure.
There's no guarantee you won't.
But what if I fall flat on my face?
Man, I've failed as many times as I've succeeded.
Get up.
Fall seven times?
Get up eight.
Failure is never final nor fatal.
Go for it!
Sail out to your dreams.

> "Twenty years from now, you will be more disappointed by the things you didn't do. Throw off the bowline. Sail from the safest harbor. Catch the wind in your sails. Explore. Dream. Discover."
>
> —Mark Twain

NOTES TO MY FUTURE SELF:

10

LIFTING THE BARN

"Hey, I've got to do this myself, and I can't do it alone."
—Anonymous

It's written into our heritage as Pineywoods people to be self-sufficient.

Our pioneer ancestors relied on themselves to get the job done.

But they weren't as self-sufficient as it seemed. It's hard to build a log cabin by yourself. Just getting the heavy logs to the homesite is an enormous job in itself.

And it's next to impossible to raise a wall of logs by yourself.

Or build a mud chimney.

It took teamwork, and that meant neighbors.

Because just one man or woman can't accomplish some jobs.
There has to be teamwork.
The old-timers called it "Neighborliness."
"I know you'll help me and I will gladly help you in return."

While n Africa, I learned an important Swahili word, *Pamoja.*
Teamwork.
Pamoja.
It was a key component of how small groups and families lived in the bush.
Pamoja.
Let's do it together.

There's a story about how neighbors can accomplish together what seems impossible.
It's called, "Lifting the Barn."
"Herman Ostry's barn floor was under twenty-nine inches of water because of a repeated rising creek flooding. The Bruno, Nebraska farmer, invited a few friends to a "barn raising." He needed to move his entire 17,000-pound barn to a new foundation over 143 feet away. His son, Mike, devised a latticework of steel tubing. Then he nailed, bolted, and welded it on the inside and the outside of the barn. Mike attached hundreds of handles.

After one practice lift, 344 volunteers slowly walked the barn up a slight incline, each supporting less than fifty pounds.

In just three minutes, the barn was on its new foundation.
Pamoja.

Together.

This statement summarizes it.

"I have to do this alone, and I can't do it by myself."

As a writer, I've learned to hand off tasks I'm not good at.

I can spend a frustrating hour on my laptop when the problem can be solved with only two keystrokes by a teenage grandson.

They're helping me lift the barn.

Writing a book is always a team effort. I live by the wise words, "A writer needs friends before he needs readers."

"One, two, three, lift."

Delegate

Allow others to help. It's incredible how many people are willing, able, and talented and love to be in on distinct steps in writing a book.

I read this, "A well-made and well-written book can change the world around it."

But I can do neither without fellow lifters.

This book you're holding, *The Three Tree*s, has hundreds of fingerprints all over it.

I *didn't* do it alone.

I *can't* do it alone.

Most great advances or products result from teamwork.

Yes, teamwork.

One, two, three, lift

Pamoja!

"Let's work together, come on, come on.
Let's work together.
You know together we will stand
Every boy, girl, woman and man."
— "Let's Work Together"
Canned Heat

NOTES TO MY FUTURE SELF:

11

L.L.L. Lifelong Learning

A small kingbird is circling the lone cedar in the heart of Dry Creek Cemetery. Knowing the kingbird's well-earned ferocious reputation, I watch for a few moments.

I'm here today for a graveside service. As it ends, the crowd slowly melts away

Soon, the only ones left are the circling kingbird and me

I doubt if any of the two dozen attendees noticed the kingbird. They've left to return to work, or life, or lost in grief.

I pay a visit to the old cedar tree in the center of the cemetery. I'm curious about why that kingbird is circling the cedar.

Curiosity. That's a big word in my vocabulary.

It goes along with being a lifelong learner.

L.L.L.

A lifelong learner.

And that lifestyle always leads to curiosity. *What is attracting the kingbird to the tree?*

I stop to take in a view of the hundreds of graves surrounding me, many of whom I knew personally or through stories.

I wonder how many lost their curiosity before they were buried here? How many died with their songs and stories still within them?

The saddest thing to see is a man or woman who has lost their curiosity or thirst for learning.

That's why I'm a lifetime member of the L.L.L. club.

I plan on learning until they put me in this dirt beneath my feet.

My attention returns to the small bird circling the lone cedar tree.

His name is *Tyrannus tyrannus.*

He's the Eastern kingbird.

Tyrannus tyrannus.

"Tyrant of all tyrants."

That's an odd genus and species name for a tiny member of the flycatcher family, but he lives up to his fierce name.

If you've watched a kingbird protect its territory, you'll understand its fitting taxonomic title. It's best known for its trait of fiercely protecting its territory. Cats and other birds are unwelcome, and the kingbird will aggressively attack any intruder.

It spends its days perching on high line wires or atop tall trees, surveying its personal kingdom.

It delights in chasing away any trespasser. It especially takes as an insult if a crow invades its domain. If you've seen a smaller bird chasing, pecking, and harassing a crow, it's likely a kingbird.

I once watched a kingbird chase a crow across an open field out of sight, far past its territory.

I believe the kingbird was having a good time.

Not so for the crow.

I enjoyed it. I love underdogs and shouted, "Get after him. Show him who's boss!"

Standing in the shade of the old cedar, I study the kingbird as it flits about. Something is going on up in the air.

I hear a strange buzzing from near the cedar tree. It sounds like a rattlesnake, but it's the humming of bees. The cedar tree is home to a huge beehive.

I'm amazed how this old wizened tree, in the last stage of a long life, is still alive *with life*.

Dry Creek Community has nursed it through hurricanes, ice storms, and the ravages of time. The cedar has lost several large limbs, but the remaining limbs keep their deep green straw.

They planted the first cedar tree beside the first grave in what became Spears Cemetery. A family, while traveling by wagon through Dry Creek, had a daughter die.

With the blessings of the Spears family, the traveled buried their young daughter, before continuing on to Texas.

They left behind one precious piece of their circle. Mr. Len Spears planted a cedar tree sapling beside the girl's grave in his field. It was the old-time way of marking a new grave to commemorate life.

The grave marker eventually rotted, but the cedar tree grew. It's still alive.

It's still filled with sap, hanging on to life.

In fact, it's the only tree in the cemetery. That's another Pineywoods tradition. The only tree planted in a cemetery is a cedar. It's not by accident that it's an evergreen. A symbolic of life beyond death.

All of us in Dry Creek dread the day when some storm topples our cedar.

But today, the cemetery cedar has new life.

A hive of honeybees.

Watching the kingbird circle the cedar tree, I remember what my birdwatching mentor, my grandfather Sid Plott, called them: "Bee Martins."

They love catching bees on the fly for a quick lunch.

This cemetery kingbird, or bee martin, had found a buffet line at the old cedar tree. I watched him capture bee after bee.

The unavoidable cycle of life and death was all around me.

I shook my head as I walked away.

Yesterday, on our drive to Dry Creek, passing through Ten Mile Community, I watched a cow licking her newborn calf.

I smiled at this simple but extraordinary act of motherhood.

Today, I'm writing in a Lafayette coffeehouse. A mother with a young baby sat near me. I went over, "That's a beautiful baby."

"Thank you."

"You're at a special time in your life."

"I know."

Walking away, I said, "Wait until you have grandkids. They're not better, but different-better."

The mother smiled. "That's what my parents say."

Just for a moment, I recalled that cow licking her newborn calf.

The amazement of new life.

The joy of being a lifelong long learner who notices.

THIS WORLD IS A WONDER.

I've always had this curiosity and wonder about life, and I've had an innate desire to write about it.

The first thing I ever wrote and showed to the light of day was a two-line poem.

I'd discovered *The Cat in the Hat*, and I guess my inner Dr. Suess was coming out:

> "This world is a wonder
> By thunder."

I proudly showed it to my parents and family. My Mom made out as if I was a young Walt Whitman as she taped it to the fridge.

I now cringe, thinking about how corny it sounded.

However, I still feel that way about the world around me.

I'm curious about it.

I want to pay attention and be amazed.

And I want to share remarkable stories about old cedars, honeybees, birds, motherhood, and the wonders of the universe.

Yes, I'm still writing that first poem,

"This world is a wonder.

By thunder."

And I'm still that curious boy.

May it always be so.

🌲

"Curiosity can be taught."
—Seth Godin

NOTES TO MY FUTURE SELF:

12

BE A READER

"Once you learn to read, you will be forever free."
—Frederick Douglas

I'm not only a writer and a lifelong learner.
I'm a lifelong *reader*.
They go together.
Reading and learning.
Reading is one of the most important habits I've incorporated into my life.

Some of my best friends are deer-stand readers. Many times they're in cell phone dead zone. They always carry a book, keeping one eye warily on the open book and the other on their deer feeder.

When they say that my books are among their favorite book deer stands reads, I take it for the great compliment it is.

These are my people. They are who I write for.

Reading.
It can be anything.
Anywhere.
Any method.
What about reading on screens? iPhones? iPads?

I read books, the news, and blogs on my phone. I can learn from a short story on either a pad or book.

Like most of you, I prefer a physical book in my hands, but that's not the direction the world is taking.

Screens.

Our phones are a great tool to learn. Siri and I have a very intimate relationship.

That's still counts as reading.

You can learn just about anything with a Google search.

Reading is reading. Scroll on but don't waste your time *doom-scrolling* and watching and thumbing through an hour of Tik-Tok-staged videos.

The Internet is a tool and, like any tool, it can be used to learn or it can be destructive. Use your fingers and mind wisely.

The medium of reading has evolved throughout history. Once humans learned how to put words and stories on cuneiform, reading has evolved and persisted as one of life's primary methods.

Read. It's a source of great joy. Read books that entertain as well as teach. Many are within the same cover.

Do audio books count?

Sure. If you're reading, you're learning.

My friend Dean is a housepainter. Headphones on, he listens to several audiobooks per week.

He's learning and enjoying.

Make your car a library.

I have friends driving the two hour round trip to the Lake Charles refineries who engross themselves in audiobooks.

It's amazing how that turns a time of tedium into a world of adventure and learning.

Be careful. I've missed my turnout several times, deep in the weeds of a good story in a gripping story.

Do audiobooks really count as reading?

Sure they do.

What should I read about?

Whatever interests you.

My reading preferences have changed.

I've graduated from reading *Field and Stream* and *Sports Illustrated* cover-to-cover, but I still feel that same joy when I hold the written word in my hand.

I keep a set of dusty encyclopedias at the Old House to remember how I learned as a child. I take a volume to the porch and leaf through it.

It takes me back, and it still has fresh things to teach me.

Ronnie Elliott grew up in Dry Creek. Like all of us in our community, he grew up poor. I never never knew we were poor until I stepped onto the real urban world, but then I also realized I was rich in the extended family and woods surrounding me.

From his childhood, Ronnie had a fascination with flying. At the old Dry Creek School, he had the teacher's permission to sprint outside to watch an airplane flying over the school.

The school librarian noted Ronnie's interest in airplanes and subscribed to *Flying* magazine. The day it arrived each month, Ronnie would hurry to the library and inhale every article, including the ads.

At sixteen, he scraped enough money to go up for a ride at the DeRidder Airport. He told me, "When stepped off that plane, I said, 'This is what I'm going to do for the rest of my life."

Ronnie has flown every type of plane from his time in Vietnam to a lifetime as a the chief fire spotter for the Forest Service.

It took root with a kindly librarian who saw Ronnie Elliott's interest and subscribed to a magazine that few rural school libraries had.

The process of reading took Ronnie Elliott from his family store to a life in the skies.

Read widely.

Scarf down books.

Always have one in your purse or on your phone.

Stories abound about the reading habits of the young Abraham Lincoln. He walked to any settlement within twenty miles to borrow books on any subject. He saved his hard-earned money to buy candles for nighttime reading.

I didn't think it's a stretch to say that his voracious appetite for books and reading led him from a log cabin to the White House.

A few words on leadership and readers.

First, everyone is a leader in some capacity, whether it's organizing the car pool or overseeing a major project at Meta.

Leader, it's important to grow as a reader so can lead more effectively.

You can be a reader and not be a leader, but you can't be a leader without being a reader.

Read on!

I read several types of leadership books.

I hunt well-written books on the principles of leadership. I'm not interested in voluminous books, but well-written practical books on the various aspects of leadership.

I read and listen to books and podcasts on writing and marketing. These keep me growing in my craft.

I read biographies. There is no better leadership lessons than following the narrative of successful growth in an individual's life-arc.

I also enjoy military history. They contain examples of heroism and courage, as well as examples of how poor leadership can cost thousands of lives.

No matter how long you've led, there are new lessons.
Above all, be a reader.
Your life will be so much richer for it.

> "A writer only begins a book.
> A reader finishes it."
> —Samuel Johnson

> "No man is poor who has a book in his pocket."
> -C.G. Terry

NOTES TO MY FUTURE SELF:

13

IF YOU LIKE PEOPLE

"If you like people, people will like you."

I saw this sign in a dusty, difficult refugee camp in Northern Uganda.

It was hand-lettered on rough cardboard.

I took a photo and moved along. I did not know that it would become one of the profound statements of my life.

"If you like people, people will like you."

It's so simple, yet so true.

It applies from among the world's poorest to the plush corner office of the Fortune 500 C.E.O.

Excuse me for peppering this mantra throughout *The Three Trees*. This book is about relationships and it can be distilled into this one sentence.

"If you like people, people will like you."

Some things are worthy of repeating.

I think of the owner of my office. It's not really my office, but it's where I work most days. It's called Tamp and Ground Coffee at the corner of 4th and DeSoto in downtown Alexandria.

I can't explain why its ambiance is so conducive to my writing. It's loud, crowded, and many of the daily clientele are what I'd call "Eccentrically Bohemian."*

But they've become my friends and I consider it my mission point.

The person who makes Tamp and Grind a happy and welcoming place is Amanda Phillips, the owner.

Amanda has a melodic voice coupled with a contagious laugh. I notice that the baristas have developed the same qualities, and it pours over into the customers.

I've observed that Amanda simply likes people and is a relationship builder.

It can't be faked and should be consistent.

As in, "If you like people, people will like you.

The concepts in *The Three Trees* boil down to relationships.

Summarized on a cardboard billboard in Rhino Camp refugee camp in northern Uganda.

"If you like people, people will like you."

*"Bohemianism is a social and cultural movement that has, at its core, a way of life away from society's conventional norms and expectations. The term originates from the French *bohème* and spread to the English-speaking world. It was used to describe mid-19th-century non-traditional lifestyles, especially of artists, writers, journalists, musicians, and actors in major European cities."
—From *Wikipedia*.

NOTES FROM MY FUTURE SELF:

14

THE 10-4-2 RULE

"It don't cost a dime to be nice to people."
—Sparky Anderson
Cincinnati Reds

In Louisiana, we are serious about how we meet people and greet each other.

We are a big-hearted people and enjoy making friends. We believe that "A Friend is just a stranger we've not met yet."

We have multiple greetings, terms of endearment, and a host of ways we show hospitality. It's not called Southern hospitality by accident. We enjoy making people feel welcome and comfortable, especially in my part of the rural Pineywoods.

I can only touch on this expansive subject. Someone ought to write a book about it, and maybe I will.

I recently read about the 10-4-2 rules. I've adjusted it to reflect "The Dry Creek Way" and want to use it as a framework for some thoughts.

The 10-4-2 rules are simple guidelines for approaching and meeting people. Everything depends on relationships, and nowhere is this more important than in how we encounter people.

At ten feet,
At four feet,
And at two feet.

TEN FOOT: THE BEGINNING.

When you're approaching someone, acknowledge them.

Show that they matter by noticing them.

Look at them. At each stage of 10-4-2, eye contact is the key.

It's a subtle way of showing respect, and Pineywoods greetings are all about respect.

You're silently saying, *Hey, I see you.*

Acknowledge that you've noticed them. They are a person worthy of not being ignored.

Then smile. Nothing lays the foundation for a positive interaction better than a smile.

Smiles. They're encounters of the best kind.

Here's a secret: smiles are contagious, and they're also infectious.

Everyone needs one, and everyone has one to give. Give one away as you approach the person. There's no quota in your heart.

Then there's the subtle art of the Southern nod. It's a non-verbal greeting between men that works similar to a smile.

A Southern nod is best defined as tipping your hat without a hat.

A simple dip of the head and chin.

And although the recipient may not even recognize it, it sends a message.

It's a hint of respect.

Respect is a key ingredient in any encounter, regardless of age, gender, or culture.

Whether it's a ten second encounter or one that lasts a lifetime.

The Southern Nod can begin at ten feet or any distance.

It speaks loudly as in, *I see you. Although we're unacquainted, I respect you as an oxygen-breathing, walking member of the human race.*

FOUR FEET: THE PAUSE

We're close enough now to show good manners and exude graciousness.

You may pass them on the cereal aisle at Walmart, but you can still bless them with some light.

It's time to ratchet up that smile.

Give them a disarming smile.

You can make your eyes smile. If you work at it, you can make your entire face smile.

That friendly, disarming smile.

I can't describe it, but everyone knows it when they receive it.

A disarming style works best in a parking lot. It's a warm smile that says, "You're safe. I'm friendly."

Words aren't necessary, but they are effective.

It's time for greetings.

We Southerners have developed it into a fine art. It's who we are. It's inherent in us, and we're naturally predisposed to it.

The sheer volume of our "Yes sirs," "No ma'ams," "Have a nice days," and "How are y'alls" is not something I'll apologize for.

Say, "Hello." It works wonders.

"Good morning."

"How are you today?"

Just make that verbal connection, step back, and see where it leads.

"How are you today, Sir?"

"Good morning, Ma'am."

A Southern man is usually polite, and this is best shown in how we address older people.

Southern men often overuse "Sir" and "Ma'am." In rural communities like Dry Creek, these elders become "Uncle" or "Aunt."

It was a sign of respect, and we embraced it.

It's still a matter of class and good raising.

Ann Landers said it well, "Class is considerate of others. It knows that good manners is more than a thing of the ancient past."

The story is told of a man holding a door open as a woman rushed by.

She said indignantly, "I'm a woman. I don't need any man to hold a door for me."

He replied. "Ma'am, I didn't hold the door because you're a woman. I held it open because I'm a *gentleman*."

Being a gentleman never goes out of style, neither does class.

If you don't have class, no matter what else you have, it won't make up for it.

I live in a racially divided city, and I've found there is power and connection in addressing all older men as "Sir" and younger men, such as "Hey, Man."

There's a glint in a man's eye when I address him as *Sir* or *Man*.

Hey man. I see you. You matter.

Sir, I respect you.

One of my friends meets older men well, especially Black men.

"I introduce myself and get their name. During the conversation I call them by name as in, 'It's nice to meet you, Mr. Jones' or 'Have a nice day, Mr. Buddy.'

"It matters not if you use their first or later name, either shows respect."

It's amazing how the smallest nuance in greeting can connect in a big way.

As Sparky Anderson said, "It don't cost a dime to be nice to people."

That's not good English, but it's good manners.

Then, we have our Louisiana terms of endearment.

Here's my two cents on it.

I'll start with a good story.

On a recent drive through my local McDonald's, the lady on the order PA said, "That'll be $6.77, Baby."

I drove to the cashier window, and the server smiled as she took my cash. "Here's your change, Hon."

To top it off, when the third window worker handed me my sausage biscuit, she said, "Here you go, Sug."

I said, "You really like people, don't you?"

She grinned. "Sug, I sure do."

I'm unsure about how to spell "sug," but I know what it means. It's a shortened term for the ultimate Southern endearment, "Sugar."

FOUR FEET TO TWO FEET

Between four and two feet, it's time to make direct eye contact.

Yes, make eye contact, but it's not a staring contest.

It's one more step in the upcoming greeting. *I see you.*

It's also a time for you to pickup some non-verbal cues. A person of grace always looks for these.

Are they looking at you or being shifty-eyed and glancing away?

Will they even look you in the eye? Are they jumping from foot-to-foot as if the floor is hot?

Where are their hands? A person's hands often tell where their emotions are.

I have an uncontrollable tic when I engage with people. I call it my Irish wink.

It's a quick mischievous wink that's accompanied by a wry smile. There's nothing sensual about it. I like to joke and josh with people and when I do, my right eye gives a playful, smiling wink.

I inherited it from my Irish ancestor, Joseph Moore. A teenage stowaway, Joe Moore settled in Sugartown after adventures in New Orleans and the No Man's Land.

He was my great-great-great grandfather and his daughter married an Iles, uniting our families.

And somehow his playful wink and ended up among his Louisiana ancestors. My own Irish wink is uncontrollable and usually occurs when I'm deep into a story or conversation.

In its own unspoken way, that wink can be a timber in bridging a new relationship.

Everyone's got some version of "Irish wink" in them. It's your job to figure out what this non-verbal cue, in you and others, really says.

TWO FEET: FACE TO FACE

These verbal greetings and non-verbal cues bring us within about two feet of our new friend.

This is the time for our various rituals of physical greeting.

Every culture has them.

Ours begins with a handshake.

A firm handshake.

My previous book, Where *Come From*, includes a chapter titled "Shake Like a Man."

I'll review it in one paragraph.

First impressions last, and a firm handshake can open doors. There's no excuse for wet rags or limp noodles. A man's handshake is an acquired habit.

Practice it.

I've noticed another subtle addition to the customary handshake.

It's the two-handed clasp. It surpasses a handshake and denotes a deeper bond of empathy and connection. A deeper eye contact accompanies that clasp. I always walk away from that clasp feeling better about myself and the world around me.

As I have traveled that wide world, I've found that every culture and tribe has its own unique, subtle clues, and greetings.

Recently, I met a young couple at Tamp and Grind Coffee in Alexandria. I immediately recognized them as from the Horn of Africa. (Somalia, Ethiopia, or Eritrea.)

I introduced myself. "Greetings. I lived three years in Uganda. You're from the Horn of Africa, aren't you?"

They beamed. Africans, whether short-termers or lifelong residents, love to connect.

The man proudly nodded. "We're from Somalia."

Then he made a subtle movement. *He lightly tapped his chest three times.*

In Somalia, that chest tap means, "We are now connected in my heart."

I returned his salute. I'd made a new friend.

He and I had not only shared greetings. We were now heart-connected.

I want to return to the important subject of eye contact.

Look a man square in the eye and maintain contact.

It shows awareness and respect.

It sends several messages.

At the moment, *You're the most important person in my world.*

Avoid distraction and nervousness; neither impress.

Avoid shifty eyes.

Don't let the ding of an Apple watch or phone ping break that connection. Each has a notification to mute your screen. Turn off the vibration. It is practically impossible to ignore that buzz on your wrist.

Once again, at this moment, the person you're with is the most important person in the world.

Show them they are by giving them your completion attention,

By briefly ignoring your screen, you convey to this person they are your top priority; you value what they have to say.

Be present. You own that Apple watch or iPhone. It doesn't own you.

You're not that important to detach for a few minutes.

PERSONAL SPACE

Everyone has personal space, and it varies. Be attentive to people's body language.

Good personal space is when you can tell their eye color but cannot count the nose hairs in their nostrils.

Simply put, you want to be close, but not too close.

As you observe their interaction, you'll actually sense the right distance.

Try it and see.

ON HUGS

The hug has evolved in my lifetime. People are much more open to hugging.

They come in various sizes. There's the short friendly hug, the bear hug, the Baptist sideways hug, the Manly hug, and more.

You need to discern whether someone wants or needs a hug. Let them take the first step.

Most folks in my culture are huggers.

I give them a short friendly hug.

Except for my grandsons. They know a Grizzly-sized bear hug is coming from their PawPaw. They've learned that resistance is futile. As they've grown into strapping young men, I've noticed that they're doing most of the hugging.

That's the power of the hug.

Many encounters will end at this point, but if they don't, it's time to chat.

People often ask, "What do I say to a stranger at my elbow during a dinner party?"

It's simple. Ask them about their life. It's not an inquisition. It's a sincere effort to learn more about that person.

People love talking about the most important things in their lives: themselves and the things they care about.

I'm curious and often say, "Wow" or "Tell me more," or "Is that so?"

Some of the finest stories I've written come from conversations like that.

Learn to ask good questions.

Work at being a good listener.

INTRODUCTIONS

All of us can improve on introductions.

This begins with introducing yourself. Speak your name in a way that shows you are proud of it. Your family gave you that name. Say it clearly.

"Hey, I'm Curt Iles."

Keep that good eye contact while you generate some small talk. Small talk is vastly underrated. Many times, it can be the foundation of a burgeoning friendship.

I won't insult you with a list of canned talking.

Just be friendly and smile. And it's okay to talk about the weather, It's a good starter, but I believe you can be creative enough to keep your own list in your pocket and mind.

Where I come from, you can approach a group of angry bikers, nod, smile, and say, "How y'all doing today, Men."

They may return your salutation with a nod and a gruff sentence, but you're now on safe ground.

There's something magical about addressing a stranger as "Man" or "Sir."

As in "Hey man, can you help me?"

I always made it a habit to address my basketball players as "Men." I call a time out with twenty seconds to go, We're down by one point and have possession. I'm down on a knee facing the players huddled around me.

"Now listen, Men. We're going to run the give-and go on the right side, then set a screen for Shannon to get the jumper in the lane. Let's do it."

The give-and-go may not win the game, but I've addressed them as men, not boys.

Using that term practice after practice, game after game, I assure them I view them as men. Remarkedly, they began to act and play like them.

What you name it is what it'll become.

"Let's go, Men."

Try using the same approach if you're passing through a group of young men. "Excuse me, Men" or "Hey guys, how's it going today?"

"Guys" or "Fellas" both work well, but nothing beats "Men."

Another area needing tuning up is introducing two people to each other.

Recently I sat by a grandson at a tennis match. His friend on the other side was scrolling away on his phone.

I nudged my grandson who didn't take the hint, so I reached across to "doom-scroller" and introduced myself.

My grandson's manners came awake, and he introduced us. "This is my PawPaw, and PawPaw, this is my good friend Bilbo Baggins."

Always make use of these cross-current introductions.

When you're in a conversation and another friend approaches, gracefully introduce them to each other. Give them some room to shake hands while drawing them into the conversation. It's called the art of connecting.

This especially true if you're in a larger group and a lone person approaches.

Believe it or not, you've just been hired as the cruise director of this circle.

What does a cruise director do? She makes everyone comfortable and ensures no one feels left out.

I saw my dear friend John Gray perform this role at his own mother's wake. As John moved around the room hugging and being kissed by older women, he was making sure no one felt left out.

One of our friends nodded. "There John is, being the cruise director at his own mother's funeral."

I nodded. "Well, it's just who he is, and that's why we love him."

I grew up in the home of the best cruise director in Beauregard Parish.

My Mom.

Mary Iles.

It comes naturally to her.

I saw this at her recent 90th birthday party. She pushed her walker around the room, greeting, laughing, and thanking everyone down to the youngest great-grandchild for coming.

When she'd made her orbit, she stopped by me, scanned the crowd, and whispered, "Do you think I missed anyone?"

All I could say was, "Momma, you are a piece of work."

She's not glad-handing or working the crowd like some politician. Momma just likes people and shows interest in their lives.

It's the same on Mom's ultramarathon excursions to Walmart. She uses a cart for support and goes down every aisle, picking up unneeded items while speaking to practically everyone.

Not all of us have the energy or personality to be John Gray or Mary Iles. But I'm convinced that all of us have the ability to make those around us comfortable.

It's the art of connecting.

Once again, "If you like people, people will like you."

Not all of are John Gray or Mary Iles, but we can all improve.

Mom told me, "When we moved to Dry Creek, I was shy and felt like an outsider."

I said, "Momma, there's not a shy bone in your body."

She squeezed my hand for emphasis. "Curt, you don't understand. I had a bashful nature. All of us Plotts are like that, but I began practicing how to meet people and introduce myself.

"Sometimes it was awkward and hard work for me, but the more I did it, the better I got."

That's how she became Queen Mary of Clayton Iles Road.

And that's how she developed her standard greeting when shaking hands. "Hello, I'm Mary Iles from Dry Creek."

Yep, Mom, *you are Mary Iles from Dry Creek and I'm proud of you.*

Later, I asked, "Momma, have you ever thought about working on a cruise ship? I've heard they're opening one on Bundick Lake."

Then she says her famous four word statement to any inside joke from me.

"Get out of here."

Before we "Get out of here" with introductions, I want to mention a skill I've seen few conversationist exhibit.

As I stated on the back cover of *The Three Trees,* this book is about relationships.

And no one I know excels better in relationship-building than my youngest son, Dr. Terry "T-Dawg" Iles.

I first noticed this when Terry was having a one-on-one conversation with a friend. Someone walked up and interrupted, just as his friend was starting a story.

When the person walked away, Terry turned to his friend. "Now, you were telling me about the ancient Hebrew scrolls they've discovered near the Arabian sea. Tell me more."

Terry had directed the conversation back to the speaker.

I asked him afterwards how he learned to do that.

"Daddy, I noticed how often I'm in a conversation and something interrupts us, the other person seldom returns to what I was saying. They simply move on, forgetting what I was sharing.

It's just good manners to re-connect the narrative. This assures the speaker of our full attention and the value we place on their words.

Wow.

It's amazing how our own children can teach us the best lessons.

Thanks, T-Dawg, for that one.

NOTES FOR MY FUTURE SELF:

15

ACTIVE LISTENING

> "It takes a great man to be a good listener."
> —Calvin Coolidge

Good conversation involves listening.

Not just lightweight listening, but the disciplined skill of being an active listener.

What does conversation mean?

Listening.

Good conversation is a series of good questions. It's incredible what people will tell you about themselves, where they live, and what they do for a living.

Then, if they are comfortable, ask, "Tell me more."

Just listen, nod your head, keep eye contact, and ask more questions. This may sound contrived, but it isn't. You cannot fake authentic listening. They don't view it as intrusive. They see it as an interest in themselves. And everyone loves talking about themselves.

Good listening isn't fake. You cannot fake interest in a person's story. I gain many story ideas from others. Often, they'll use a word or phrase in my journal that may bloom into a full-bloom story.

"I had a wonderful time I time talking with him. He is a great conversationist."

Recently, I've read several excellent books on active listening. They are the top-rated books on Amazon.

Learn to be a better listener.

It is a skill. Like any skill, it can be improved.

"There is a way of listening that exceeds all compliments."

—Anonymous

NOTES TO MY FUTURE SELF:

16

THE SWEETEST SOUND

*N*ames.

Hearing someone call your name is the world's most delightful sound.

They have just proven that you are alive. That at this moment, they matter. Though seven billion humans inhabit the planet, you've addressed them personally.

You're saying, "You are somebody who matters."

At least to that person who took the trouble to know your name.

Something happens when we address a person by name.

I'm known for my ability to recall names. If you knew how many names I've flubbed, you would laugh at the assertion.

But it is a *skill* I've worked hard at.

And mark my words. it requires hard work. Discipline and focus.

Here are several steps to help

Say their name repeatedly in your conversation.

Be authentic, but repeat their name throughout the conversation.

Ask them something specific about their name.

Repeat their name as you part. "It was great meeting you, Frodo."

This may sound as if you're overdoing it. But remember, it is the *sweetest* sound.

Then here's the real secret to learning (and remembering names): As soon as you walk away, write down their name. Put it on a piece of paper, napkin, or even your hand.

Then, note the name in your journal and mention something specific about the person and where you met.

If I write it down, there's a much better chance I'll recall it later when needed.

Combining a greeting with their name always elicits a smile.

You've noticed.

I'm somebody.

Somebody to you.

But it's hard work.

One must develop this into a habit.

But it's worth it.

Like I said, it's the sweetest sound in the world.

Names matter even if it's a hero, a horse, and his faithful sidekick.

The Lone Ranger says, "Yes, Tonto. The guys in the white hats always win."

Tonto nods, "Yes, Kemosabe."

The Lone Ranger turns and puts his spurs to his horse, "Hi Yo, Silver, away."

As I said, names really do matter.

NOTES FOR MY FUTURE SELF:

17

THE POWER OF A HAND-WRITTEN NOTE

Writing and receiving handwritten notes and letters are relics of the past.

Things that are rare become extremely valuable in the currency of life.

Writing and receiving handwritten notes and letters are relics of the past.

That's why the power of the handwritten note has never been more valuable.

I call it being high-touch in a high-tech world.

There are so many reasons to send a note: Gratitude, encouragement, comfort.

There are stationary cards for every need.

I have postcards with my contact information. The rest of the card is blank for a note and address.

It only takes five minutes to write a heart-written note, if you make your tools convenient.

A card.

A pen.

A stamp.

You can find anyone's address using Google.

Write that note.

Stamp it.

Send

It takes a few minutes, but will be treasured for a lifetime.

Recently, I met a former student from my earlier years as a high school teacher. He pulled out his wallet and handed me a dog-eared letter I'd written him years ago. The fact that he had kept this short handwritten note reminded me of the power of personal correspondence.

This note, sent during a difficult period in his life, still meant something to him decades later.

Connecting.

John Maxwell calls this ability to build relationships "The Law of Connection." Maxwell wisely counsels, "You can't move people to action unless you first move them with emotion. The heart comes before the head."

There are many ways to build relationships by connecting with others' hearts, and one of the best is to write short handwritten notes.

"High tech, yet high touch"

This "high tech/high touch" balance is essential in our lives.

In his excellent book, *The Tipping Point*, author Malcolm Gladwell shares how the explosion of e-mail and computer-generated communication has created a need for personal correspondence. He writes, "The fact that anyone can e-mail us for free creates immunity . . . and makes us value face-to-face communications all the more."

That's why a note or phone call connects so deeply.

I communicate primarily through texts, e-mail and the telephone, which are quick and efficient ways to stay in touch. However, when I really want to thank someone or express a deep thought or inspiration, I get out a pen, a small card, and an envelope. Notes forge deeper connections, creating cherished keepsakes that people reread many times.

The time spent personally encouraging and thanking others is not wasted but instead invested. Some may say they cannot afford to spend this time, but I reply that they cannot afford not to.

Notes of appreciation

The writer of Proverbs wrote in chapter 3:27, "Do not withhold good from those who deserve it when it is in your power to act."

When we have the opportunity and words to bless someone, we should express our gratitude, concern, or encouragement freely.

A quote from Mark Twain comes to mind, "I can live for six weeks on one good compliment."

Former President George H. W. Bush was known as a great note-writer. He followed up virtually every contact with a cordial response. One surprised person received a warm, calligraphic pat on the back after lending Bush an umbrella.

We live in a high-tech world and that's not a bad thing. I can post a blog that can be read instantly on any continent.

It's a world of screens.

All of us are high-tech, (except for one of my brother-in-laws) but I firmly believe we can still be high-touch.

High tech/High touch.

That's why something written by your hand carries such weight.

It's high-touch.

Write a note

Do it today.

NOTES TO MY FUTURE SELF:

18

FRIEND-KEEPING

"Curt, you can't have too many friends."
—The lifelong adage of my mother, Mary Iles

I met two of my best friends before I started grade school, David Cole and Don Barrett.
They're my lifetime friends.
Lifetime. The best kind there is.

Here is a marker of lifetime friendships: You're always comfortable in each other's presence, and even if you haven't crossed paths recently, the minute you sit down together, you take up right from where you were last time.

That's how lifetime friends are, and that's how I feel about David Cole and Don Barrett.

They both live in Dry Creek on family land.

David Cole is a respected expert saddle maker.

Don Barrett is a beloved pastor, loved and known by everyone.

They are quite different.

Each serves the Lord in his own respective ways, but both are ministers.

Everyone knows Bro. Don Barrett. He is an extremely well-known and respected *minister* throughout SW Louisiana. He is a wonderful pastor and preacher, who has spent a lifetime ministering in churches throughout the Pineywoods.

He has preached literally hundreds of funerals in our part of the Pineywoods. That binds him to the hearts of so many people.

Don's ministry is to be out among people. He's easy to know and love. He's real and authentic.

***

My other lifetime friend, David Cole, is quieter in his life and faith. He prefers to serve in the background.

David serves on the Dry Creek Cemetery Board. His *ministry* is helping families during their emotional time of burying a loved one. He helps families select their gravesites when death comes, and is the When there's a burial at the cemetery, David is present, always standing quietly away from the crowd, observing to see if anything needs doing.

I call David's cemetery ministry a "Sacred Duty." If you've ever stood in David's spot, you'd understand my use of this term.

He has a quality that all three of the Cole brothers have: he's rock-solid.

Both Don and David are servant-leaders, and are my lifetime friends.

"The man who still his childhood friends is a rich man indeed."

Friend making.
Friend collecting.
and *Friend keeping.*
You can't separate the three.
They seem to always walk hand-in-hand.

In my previous book, *Where I Come From*, I shared thoughts about friend collectors. Those people collect friends as iron filings are attracted to a magnet.

They understand that "A stranger is just a friend you've not met yet."

They understand everything rises and falls on relationships.

In the end, it's all about relationships.

When it's all said and done, the people around us are all that matters.

When you break it down, whatever you do is built on relationships. It doesn't matter if you're a working mom, salesman, CEO, teacher, pastor, or the greeter at Walmart—you're in the business of building relationships.

Those who spend a lifetime nurturing friendships and relationships are the happiest people.

We were created to make bonds and bridges with others.

In his memorable book, *The Tipping Point*, Malcolm Gladwell defines a group of people called "connectors." These are folks who seem to know everyone and go through life making friends and contacts.

One of the joys of their lives is connecting people together, as in "I've got a friend whom you must meet; they also raise border collies."

Connectors are relationship builders.

Relationships.

It's a powerful word and should be a priority in our lives.

In every direction.

In every way.

Connecting.

That's what I love best about my closest female friend, Debra Tyler.

Her winning smile, kind spirit, and love of life always makes everyone smile.

Deb, her husband Frank, and I share the common bond of rural upbringings, love of nature and the outdoors.

Birds, trees, and the outdoors are the staple in our friend connection. We stay in touch about whip-poor-wills, honeysuckle, rainfall totals, longleaf pines, and Bundick Swamp.

Most of all, we share a deep love of Jesus. There is no bond stronger than that.

We've also stood shoulder to shoulder through the tragedies and trials of life.

I'm thankful to God for my best country-girl-friend, Debra Tyler.

FRIEND-COLLECTING

I've always been a friend-collector.

It's who I am.

More importantly, I've been a friend-keeper.

Some of my best friends today I met at East Beauregard High School and Louisiana College.

I learned about the art of friend-keeping at the feet of two of the most important people in my life: Clayton and Mary Iles.

Mom: "Curt, you can't have too many friends."

Dad's winsome smile, "Hey, it's great to meet you."

Each season and step of my life, I've made new friends.

You cannot have ongoing friendships with everyone you meet, but there should be friendships you've kept from every stage.

That describes my best friend James.

We met in college and because of sports, duck hunting, and managing church camps, we've kept our friendship fresh and alive.

We've stood beside during the most traumatic events of our lives.

January 1995
Lafayette, Louisiana

I sat with James on a critical day when his wife Shannon, pregnant with their third child, suffered a brain aneurysm.

Her condition was critical. They moved her to four hospitals before a neurosurgeon flew in from South Carolina to perform the delicate brain surgery that saved Shannon's life.

That third child, Neil, was delivered by C-section the next day.

I don't remember the details of that day. I just showed up and sat by my friend as the crisis passed over a three-day period.

James routinely brings up that day and my presence in the ICU waiting room and hospital.

It was the simple ministry of presence. That's what best friends do.

James has been present for the most turbulent times in my life.

When I've sunk into the darkness of depression, James has always been there for me. Even when I didn't want anyone around, James pushed in and gave me what I needed: the presence I so desperately needed. He helped me to hold onto the rope of hope when I felt it slipping through my hands.

The gift of presence.

That's what best friends do.

And the best friends are lifetime ones.

The friendships you keep.

To my knowledge, I've never lost a friend.

That's a lot to say for a former high school principal and African *Mzungu*.

I spoke of it earlier in Chapter 13. "If you like people, people will like you."

It's the most effective billboard I've seen, even if someone hand-lettered it on a refugee camp sign.

It's so effective that I've never forgotten it. I've paid lots of good money for leadership conferences and relational books, but "If you like people, people will like you," sums up everything I believe about relationships.

That African sign profoundly affected me, and I think of it often. I wonder where the refugee- author of the sign is today.

I know he or she would have made a good friend. I also wonder what that wandering refugee would think of his sign traveling around the world far beyond Sub-Saharan Africa.

Hopefully into your heart as it did mine.

Friendships.

That's friend-making.

Friend-collecting.

Friend-keeping.

Each can, and should be, on everyone's life-checklist.

Here's to Friendship.

Long may it run.

NOTES TO MY FUTURE SELF:

19

Grit

> "I am not the most successful or most talented person in the world, but I succeeded because I kept going, and going, and going."
> -Sylvester Stallone

Grit. What is it?

Grit wears many hats.

Resolve.

Perseverance; "Determination of firm or fixed intention to achieve a desired end."

That's Grit.

I also like this definition of Grit: "Firmness of mind or spirit. Unyielding courage in the face of hardship or danger."

Often Grit means holding our ground.

Making a stand.

It's Gandalf the Wizard, in *The Lord of the Rings*, standing astride the bridge of Khazad-Dhum opposing a balrog fire demon.

The Wizard stamps his staff. "You shall not pass here."

"You shall *not* pass *here*."

It's Colonel George Taylor on D-Day at Omaha Beach, standing tall amidst withering German fire. "Men, get up and let's move. There are only two kinds of men on this beach: those that are dead, and those that are gonna be. Come on. Let's go."

It's moving ahead when the going gets tough.

Onward.

Jesus set his face.
"He steadfastly set his face to go to Jerusalem."
—Luke 9:51

I never tire studying the life of Jesus. Not only do I follow him as Savior, he's also my Hero and lifetime Mentor. He's was a Man's kind of Man. I take issue with anyone who speaks of him as weak and wimpy.

I've always been fascinated with an overlooked passage during Jesus' week before his crucifixion. Here's the full verse in Luke 9.51,

"Now it came to pass when the time had come for Him to be received up; he steadfastly set his face to go to Jerusalem."

Don't miss the nuance of Luke's narrative.

Jesus begins his final journey toward Jerusalem:
He's got a tough job to do when he gets there.
Notice the words.
It was *time*.
He *steadfastly set his face*.
His destination: Jerusalem.
Jesus gritted his teeth and set his jaw for the journey toward his approaching cruel death on a cruel cross.
He set his face.
That's grit.
You can see it in the tight jaw and focused eyes of a man or woman when they've made up their mind to do a tough or dangerous assignment.
You can watch it in their walk as they stride forward.
That was my Jesus.

I heard a speaker recently refer to it as "DQ."
"Don't quit."
Grit is simply the refusal to quit.
Grit just won't quit.
It rhymes, but it's also true.
Grit is Resolve.
It's a good word to have in our toolbox.
Resolve.
I have a small black journal on my shelf titled on the front cover, "Resolve" and the back, "Grit."

It's full of the quotes and snippets found I've gathered often the years. I've often pulled the journal from the shelf when I've needed encouragement to stay the course. When I've needed to set my face.

Make a pocket-sized resolve book. It'll be there when you need it.

Jay is a passionate missionary who whom we served with in Africa. Before coming to the Dark Continent, he'd spent a decade sharing Christ deep in the Amazon jungles.

Jay was *a missionary's missionary.*

He was also a *barefoot missionary.* It's a respectful term missionaries use for those who live and learn amongst people in remote areas.

Jay was the only Southern Baptist missionary I've known who was *tatted up.* His arms were covered with tattoos of scripture, tribal names, and an image of his wife Susan.

One particular tattoo that always caught my attention were on his knuckles:

Four letters. One letter per knuckle. H-O-L-D-F-A-S-T.

When he placed his fists together, it clearly stated, "Hold Fast."

It defined the missionary he was. He held fast in tough places where only the brave would venture.

Hold Fast.

He held out when others pulled out their stakes.

I've been thinking about Jay's Hold-Fast-Fist tattoo.

I can't recalls if when he puts his fist puts together did the two words face him or the reader?

In other words, were "Hold Fast" for himself or for us?

Either way, I believe it was both of us.

Perseverance.

Staying the course.

Grit.

Perseverance.

Journeys, against all odds, are about perseverance.

It's about staying the course.

Having grit.

It's about not quitting on your friends.

Nor your family.

Definitely, nor your faith

Yourself. Don't quit on yourself. Or Your dreams. Or Integrity.

No turning back.

No turning back.

No retreat.

> "No retreat, no surrender."
> —Bruce Springsteen

Grit and endurance

It's Admiral Chester Nimitz in 1945, the last year of the Pacific, "We will all of us put our shoulders to the wheel and finish the job as soon as we can."

Shoulders to the wheel.

Finish the job.

Keep your hands on the plow. Don't dare look back.

Yes, that's perseverance.

Some call it persistence.

I call it grit.

Persistence

Nothing In the World can take the place of persistence. Talent will not; Nothing is more common than unsuccessful men with talent. Genius will not; Unrewarded genius is almost a Proverb. Education will not; The world is full of educated derelicts. Persistence and Determination alone are omnipotent. The slogan "Press On" has solved and always will solve the problems of the Human Race."

—Calvin Coolidge

"Do your duty;
You can do no more;
You should never do less."
—Robert E. Lee

NOTES TO MY FUTURE SELF:

20

Dream Stealers and Joy Killers

> "Somebody poisoned the water well."
> —Woody
> "Toy Story"

They're out there waiting for you.

Dream-stealers and joy-killers.

They'll poison your water well.

Run as fast as you can from them.

Sadly, they'll usually find your forwarding address and hunt you down.

That's what dream stealers and joy killers try to do.

They want to track you down and pour a bucket of cold water on your joy or dream.

Don't let them derail your dream.

I once read of a college student who turned in an assignment in a business management class. The topic was, "What I plan to do after college?"

The student labored all weekend on his paper. His dream was to start a horse farm back in his rural county. He laid out his plans and drawings in detail.

He handed in the paper on Monday.

The instructor returned the graded assignments later that week.

He'd received a D minus. Red ink blots marred the professor's paper. The teacher had written in bold letters:

THIS IS <u>NOT A</u> BUSINESS PLAN FOR A HORSE FARM! THIS PROJECT IS NOT FEASIBLE!

At the end of class, the student approached the professor, and handed his paper to the professor. "Sir, here's my paper. You can keep your D-minus, and I'll keep my dream."

He had pushed past a dream stealer in his path, refusing to be stone-walled.

Todd Graves's story on the startup of his first Raising Cane's restaurant is a similar story to our horse rancher.

Todd turned in his business paper. The professor smirked. "A restaurant that *only* serves Chicken Fingers?"

Todd's business plan received the lowest grade in class.

The professor said it wouldn't work.

Banks refused loans to Todd, but he remained undeterred. No dream killer and joy stealer was stopping him.

It takes hard work and sacrifice to make a dream come alive.

On the Road

Todd traveled to Los Angeles to work as a boilermaker at an oil refinery, grinding through ninety-hour weeks to raise the money to fuel his restaurant dream.

Learning from a fellow boilermaker that he could earn even more money commercial fishing, Todd traveled to Alaska. He camped out on the tundra for a month before landing a job on a boat fishing for sockeye salmon, working 20-hour days in harsh conditions.

Returning to His Roots

Todd returned home to Baton Rouge with his hard-earned money. Coupled with an SBA loan, he had enough to start building his restaurant near the LSU campus.

After finally getting the cash registers to work, Raising Cane's opened on August 28th, 1996. It was past 9 pm and Todd went out on the street to wave customers in. Business was so good, the restaurant stayed open 'til 3:30 am.

Todd planned to call the Restaurant "Sockeye's" as a tribute to his time in Alaska. He took a friend's advice instead, naming it after his Labrador Retriever, Cane, who often visited the construction site."

Raising Cane's.
And as they say, the rest is history.
Todd Graves's dream stealers and joy killers didn't stop him. He was willing to do what true achieving-dreamers do: put in the time and sweat needed to get the ball rolling."*

Becoming a full-time writer.
When DeDe and I made the step to my becoming a full-time writer, it was a dream come true-leap-of-faith.

I wouldn't call those who questioned this move as dream stealers. Most of them meant well.

"Are you sure this is what God wants you to do?"

"What if it doesn't work out?"

"You've got a great job. Why would you want to do something crazy like this?"

I still followed my dream. Over the last twenty-five years, I've published fifteen books.

It has been one of the most fulfilling times in my life.

I'm glad I stepped out and followed my dream.

It wasn't always easy, but it has been good.

In the earlier chapter, "Sail On," I shared about our decision to leave everything behind in Dry Creek for a three-year sojourn to Africa.

Once again, people questioned our sanity.

Some dream-stealers showed up at our front door.

We went to Africa and experienced one of the most meaningful times in our lives.

It wasn't easy.

Most of the time, it was difficult.

But we followed our dream.

🌰

"Envy is the killer of joy."
-Mark Twain

Just a few word on word on joy-killers.

They can't stand seeing someone happy, joyful, and successful. Joy Stealers are the first cousins-once-removed of dream-stealers and often travel together.

They live to pour water on anyone's exuberant joy.

🌰

My niece, whom I adore, went through a painful divorce.

She was living back home in the desert at the dead end of Clayton Iles Road.

Not a good place to meet a good man.

And that's when she met him.

It was an unusual long distance relationship.

As they fell in love on iPhone and Facetime, she kept it to herself.

Then she announced to our family that she was in love and would soon go to Florida to meet her man.

I only had one bit of advice for her: "Don't let anyone steal your joy."

There are plenty of people who love pouring cold water on things, especially an unusual romance like this. I knew they'd be waiting.

They are joy-killers.

The announcement of their impending marriage shocked many.

I saw her a few weeks before their 2024 wedding, I whispered, "You're the happiest I've seen you in years. You've got your joy back. Don't let anyone steal it.

She smiled. "I won't/"

She and her daughter made a giant leap when they moved to Florida. A couple attempting one of life's toughest challenges: blending two families with children into one.

It hasn't been easy.

Most things like this aren't.

They've been married for a year and a half. On her last visit to Dry Creek, I sidled up to her and whispered, "You've still got that joy, haven't you?

She nodded, "I sure do, Uncle Curt. I still have my joy."

Don't let those joy-killers get to you.

Avoid those dream-stealers like the plague.

They're both toxic and contagious.

My advice: run like hell.

*"Raising Canes" From https://www.raisingcanes.com/who-we-are -

NOTES TO MY FUTURE SELF:

21

Coasting

Here's what will happen if you don't have a life plan.
You'll coast.
We'll talk more about having a life plan in Chapter 38.
Without a plan, you'll fall prey to "Mission drift."
In sports, we call it "Game slippage."
You'll get in a rut.
Please don't coast.
"Lord, don't let me get too comfortable."
It's a good prayer for any of us.
It's one of the saddest things to see. A leader, teacher, construction worker, anyone.
A person who has lost their drive.

They're just hanging on.
Waiting for retirement.
Lost their fire.
Burnt out.

I'm in the season of my life where it'd be easy to get comfortable.
Too comfortable.
To give in and coast to the finish line.
I need to challenge myself daily.
The opposite of coasting is seeking higher ground,
You can't coast uphill.
Keep moving up. Onward.
The antidote to coasting is to keep moving up. Learning. Growing stretching.
Learn something new.
Move to something else.
Rearrange your office and desk.
Tear up your teaching notes and start again.
Whatever it takes, choose not to coast.
It is a decision.
Make the right one.

I have a friend who is a funeral director. He told me of category that sometimes goes on death certificates: Adult Loss of Vigor.
Adult Loss of Vigor.
I asked, "What is that?"
"It's when an older person just basically gives up and withers and dies."
Loss of Vigor.

Giving up on life.

Resist the urge to bury yourself in a safe cocoon and simply be comfortable.

I'm not complaining about the comforts of life in the 21st century. I enjoy AC, Wi-Fi, and What-A-Burger as much as the next guy.

But I have a healthy fear of getting too comfortable.

Instead of being comfortable, I wish to be content.

These two C words are very different.

My wife, DeDe, shared about our sojourn in Africa with our Bible study group.

Someone asked, "How did it feel to sell your house and possessions and journey to another continent?"

DeDe's reply was succinct, "I've never been more content in my life."

Contentment is living happily with what you have and who you are.

In a comfort zone, we can get too comfortable, ease off the gas pedal, take no chances, and become lazy.

And laziness is much more than physical.

There's spiritual laziness.

There's intellectual laziness.

And there's emotional laziness.

All are bad. None are good.

As I look in the mirror each morning, I need to ask myself three questions:

What is my comfort zone?

What do I need to do to get out of my comfort zone?

What am I going to do about it?

I hope you are contented, but not too comfortable.

Onward!

NOTES TO MY FUTURE SELF:

22

Ruts

"Choose your rut carefully: you'll be in it for the next mile."
-Handmade sign at the turnoff on the highway to our Old House.
(circa 1960.)

"A rut is nothing but an open grave with both ends open."

I grew up down Clayton Iles Road.
Notice I said down, not on.

Our road turned west off Highway 113, several miles south of Dry Creek.

It was a dirt, one-mile-long dead-end road.

That's significant to who I am.

In my boyhood, it was a nameless road.

A straight one-mile dirt road.

Muddy during wet weather and rutted up.

Rutted up,

Only someone who's driven a dirt road after a rainstorm can understand the power and importance of ruts.

I think often of those hand-lettered sign, "Choose your rut carefully . . ."

That sounds like the start of another good story. *Choose your rut carefully.*

On Clayton Iles Road (which became signed in my adulthood.) ruts had a great deal with getting stuck.

A dead-end road has its own personality. When we'd hear traffic crunching along the gravel, we knew one of two things was true: they were coming to see us or were lost.

Living at the end of a dead-end road gives one perspective. It's where it all started for me.

It's so easy to get in a rut in our lives.

It's not easy to dig out of one. Here are some starters:

Recognize and admit you're in a rut.

Decide to do something about.

Write down three ruts in your life as well as three decisions to change.

Get out of your routine.

Do something different.

As a teacher, I'd rearrange my classroom at least once each semester. I'd change the location of my desk and all of my books.

The change seemed to invigorate the students, but it most affected me.

It was a fresh look and new day.

I'd crawled out of that specific rut.

You can do the same.

NOTES TO MY FUTURE SELF:

23

THE MINISTRY OF PRESENCE

Showing up when people are hurting is called *the ministry of presence.*

I'll delve into the terms "Ministry" and "Minister" later.

But first, a story.

I sit closely beside Mike. I want to touch him and feel the life in him I want to touch him so he can feel the love I have for him.

Mike King has fought a long battle with cancer.

Last week, he left the complex of M.D. Anderson Cancer Center in Houston to come home to Dry Creek.

He's come home to die.

I can't of a better place to make a last stand than Dry Creek, Louisiana.

I've never *not known* Mike King. That's not good English, but it's the truth. He was six years older than me and I looked up to him.

I still do.

My dad, Clayton Iles, was a key mentor and example to Mike as a youth.

Ed King, Mike's father played those same roles in my life.

It's the beauty of growing up in a place called Dry Creek.

Since coming home, a constant flow of friends and family have showered Mike with expressions of deep love.

He is a rock solid beloved member of our community.

Once again, "If you love people, people will love you."

It's so true for my friend Mike.

I will say this about Big C.

Cancer gives you a chance to have a long goodbye.

And Mike King is taking in the love showered upon him in his long goodbye.

I tell his wife Debbie, "I know he's on hospice, but he's invigorated."

Getting him out of that hospital and back to Ed King Road has made a huge difference.

His body is weakening, but his spirit is soaring. You can see it in his eyes and feel it around him.

It's called love, and it's the most powerful medicine in the world.

I sit beside him. "Mike, you look better than you did last week. I believe you've still got some sap left in you."

We laugh. We both know he's dying, but he's finishing strong and with bravery.

"I also believe you've got some miles left on your odometer."

We laugh again. Death is too serious not to laugh at.

But everyone in Mike's circle has shed plenty of tears. That's also part of the long goodbye.

Several people have said, "Well, I'd go see, Mike but I wouldn't know what to say" or "I drove by there but there were too many cars there."

Man, go park on the grass, go in and kiss Mike King on the top of the head, even if he's asleep, and hug his wife Debbie.

Even if you don't say a word, you've just performed the *ministry of presence.*

Ministry.

The ministry.

Called to the ministry.

A minister.

We've cloaked this word ministry/minister in clerical collars. "He's called to the ministry" or "He's a minister of the gospel."

But listen to these definitions below:

Ministry. "De an Instrument used to . . ."

Minister: "Someone who attends to the needs of another." i.e. "Her doctor was busy ministering to the injured."

We're all ministers and you don't need a certificate of ordainment to do that.

All you have to do is show up and care.

In spite of grief, tragedy, illness, and disaster, in spite of your own fear, show up.

Show up and *minister.*

I don't know how much longer Mike King will live. It's often hard to beat Big C.

But as I looked at my friend on the couch surrounded by siblings, children, grandchildren, and a host of lifetime friends, I thought,

That man's not dying. He's living. At this moment, he's more alive than he's probably ever been. That's what an outpouring of love does to man.

I'm not naive. In the end, Big C will win. It often does.

But in the meantime, I want to spend special time holding his elbow.

That's the ministry of being there.

The ministry of presence. A task that every human can perform.

Go!

In spite of your fear, just go.

Mike King is on hospice but he's holding his own as this book goes to print. I hope to present a copy to him.

I told him he might be like Jimmy Carter and stay on hospice for a year.

Here's one more bit of advice.
I wrote this part of the story long before Mike's illness.
Go to the funeral.
Yes. You heard me.
Go to the funeral. When there's a death among your family or friends, acknowledge it.

There are many ways to personally commemorate a special person's life and death.
Human nature is that we avoid death.
It's awkward.
We don't like to mention it at all if possible.
We don't like to admit it's real.
We avoid it.
But death, excuse the pun, is part of life.
That's why it's so important to step out of our comfort zone and show compassion.
Go to the funeral or the wake.
Your loved one or friend will never forget that you were there.
You showed up.
A older country woman once told me, tears in her eyes, "I can still name every person who came to Daddy's funeral and it was twenty years ago."
Once again, the ministry of presence.
It's the showing up that matters.
I often hear the excuse, "Well, I'd go, but I don't know what I'd say."
At that moment, people don't need words. They need the presence of a friend or group of friends gathering around them.
In fact, the less you say, the better.
Keep it simple.

"I'm sorry for your loss."

"I love you, and you know how much I loved your Momma."

"I care for you."

Then shut your mouth, give them a big hug, and move aside so others can express their condolences.

You are practicing the ministry of presence. Resist the urge to use irritating platitudes such as "God just needed another flower" or "You'll get over this with time."

Shut your trap!

Keep it simple.

Hug them. Shake their hand and say, "I love you. I care for you. I'm here for you. I'm praying for you."

You can bring great comfort to the grieving.

On February 1, 2003, the Space Shuttle Columbia came apart above East Texas, and the long search for remains of the astronauts and pieces of wreckage dragged on for weeks.

Soon, NASA mailbags filled with letters of appreciation, support, and encouragement, mostly from children, arrived at the collection centers and at the Johnson and Kennedy Space Centers.

They were basically unanimous in their sentimental messages. *We're sorry for your loss. We're praying for you. We believe in you. Keep flying.*

Oftentimes, time, distance, and opportunity will prevent your presence.

There are numerous ways to express your sympathy from afar. Flowers, a memorial gift, sympathy card, or handwritten note are always appreciated.

Phone calls may seem difficult. Once again, just speak from your heart. "I was thinking of you and your family and I wanted to . . . "

A phone call. There's something deeply connective about hearing an empathetic voice on the other end.

I've found that the grieving appreciate a call or text several weeks after the funeral, assures them that they and their loved one haven't been forgotten.

Even a heartfelt text beats silence.

I always record birthdays and death dates on my phone calendar with a reminder alert. It only takes a moment to text, "Hey, it's your Daddy's birthday today. I know you miss him badly and so do I."

All of these small acts of kindness are multiplied at a time of death.

Go to the funeral.

If you can't, do something.

It's the Pineywoods way.

NOTES TO MY FUTURE SELF:

24

HIGH EXPECTATIONS

"I have to live with myself, and I want to be fit to live with."
– Edgar Guest

It begins with high expectations of yourself.

You expect the best daily.

You won't coast or just mail it in.

You can look in the mirror and know you're becoming the best version of yourself you can become.

Then channel those high expectations to others.

As a young leader, I discovered a powerful tool for leading young people. At the end of a long workday, a tired group of teenage staffers surrounded me and I'd assign the next day's tasks.

I'd always end with, "I want to thank you in advance for doing this."

It had a magical effect. Whether to a single worker or a group, they responded to "I want to thank you . . ." the result was a completed job done well.

I was learning the power of high expectations. If you expect the best of others, you'll usually get it.

I also realized another thing: people don't like to let us down.

They don't want to disappoint you, especially when you're depending on them.

The best leaders I worked for made it clear what they wanted and got out of your way to let you do it.

They trusted me.

I would've crawled on broken glass not to disappoint them.

They don't have to scream or push his weight around.

He led by the power of high expectations.

Always have high expectations for yourself.

Have high expectations for others and trust them to do the assigned job.

"The chief lesson I have learned in a long life is that the only way you can make a man trustworthy is to trust him; and the surest way to make him untrustworthy is to distrust him."
—Henry Stimson, Secretary of War during World War II.

NOTES TO MY FUTURE SELF:

25

A Woman Named Lou

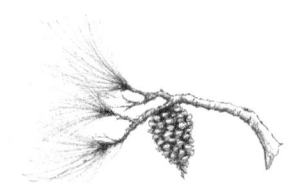

Her name is Lou.

I hope one day you get to meet her.

I've known Lou all of her life, and I've seldom seen her get bent out of shape.

We grew up together and I can honestly say I've never seen Lou offended, set off-kilter, or lose her cool.

She's unflappable.

Her low-key personality contrasts with the way she played basketball. She was an All-State guard who went on to play in college. She played basketball with a burning passion, always on the move with cat-like quickness, ready to drive the lane with no fear.

But she never changed expression.

No bad call or hard foul seemed to affect her.

I loved watching her play.

That was decades ago. She no longer sprints the length of the court. Old point guards usually end up with bad knees.

But she's still unoffendable.

Not perfect, but always cool.

She seems to be the unoffendable woman.

That's a good title to have.

What is the mark of an unoffendable life?

It's the mark of a person who doesn't easily get bent out of shape. They don't carry a chip on his or her shoulder. They let offenses roll off their back and choose to overlook slights, real or imagined.

The unoffended person chooses not to hold grudges. She understands that there is no heavier load to carry than a grudge.

She has prized relationships above harsh words or hurt feelings.

The unoffended woman is good-natured. She's chosen to develop the habit of being cheerful.

Webster's defines *good-natured* as "having a pleasant disposition and displaying an easygoing manner, especially in social situations."

An unoffended person oozes *graciousness*.

Listen to Paul's words in Colossians 4:6: *Let your speech always be gracious, seasoned with salt, so that you may know how you ought to answer each person.*

You ask, "What is the definition of graciousness?"

Webster's defines it as "Carrying oneself well in every situation."

You'll definitely know it when you see it.

And a lack of graciousness is also hard to miss.

True graciousness has nothing to do with wealth, class, background, or race.

Graciousness and class.

Two good words that always seem to travel together.

Like graciousness, class has nothing to do with status.

"Class speaks of an aristocracy that has nothing to do with ancestors or money. The most affluent blue-blood can be totally without class, while the descendants of a Welsh Miner, may ooze class from every pore."

How you look at something goes a long way toward being unflappable and unoffendable.

The confident, unoffended person doesn't have to get in the last word. Sometimes, she bites off her tongue, knowing that often the best answer to ignorance is silence.

Because silence can speak volumes.

Living an unoffended life is not a sign of weakness. It doesn't entail being run over, pushed around, or exploited. It is a sign of inner strength and peace.

There's no chip on her shoulder.

She attempts to cut people slack, remembering that folks often act a certain way because they have an ingrown toenail.

Richard Carlson's excellent book *Don't Sweat the Small Stuff (and It's All Small Stuff)* speaks of this concept of being unflappable. "They don't sweat the small stuff. The unoffendable person overlooks the minor irritations of life."

Like I said, you'd like Lou.

Lou inherited that unflappability from her father, whom I also knew very well.

He was like that, too. He was a gracious and unoffended man, always comfortable in his own skin. He would've been the same man visiting the Oval Office as he was at Foreman's Grocery.

He was a "What you see is what you get kind of man" and that's a trait highly admired among Pineywoods people.

You also would have loved Lou's dad. Everyone did. He died having not a single enemy on the earth.

Yes, he was also unoffendable.

Just like his daughter.

Me? Unoffendable?

I'm still working on it.

I have a way to go in being unoffendable or unflappable, but I'm trying.

I really am.

"Sensible people control their temper; they earn respect by overlooking wrongs."

—Proverbs 19:11 NLT

"Show class, have pride, and display character. If you do, winning takes care of itself."

—Bear Bryant

NOTES TO MY FUTURE SELF:

26

Choose Your Hill Carefully

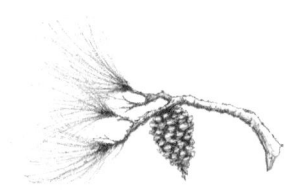

"A brindle cur dog can whip a skunk, but it's still not a good idea."
—Lloyd Iles

It's true. A good cur dog can whip a skunk any day of the week. However, a smart one won't.

It's simple: you can win a fight and still lose.
Pick your battles.
And pick them carefully.
Conversely, if a fellow wants to, he can get into a fistfight every day.
There's always someone ready to take you on.
You can have an ongoing "hip-hop beef" if you choose.

They never end; only escalate.

Ask Drake and Kendrick Lamar.

Having a beef.

There are folks out there who'll be glad to join you.

We make a choice daily. All day long. Will we get along with others, or will we carry a chip on our soul? (Or is it shoulder? or can it be both?)

We make a choice about how we'll react to the person who cuts us off in traffic or blares their horn.

It's a choice.

We must choose what hill to die on.

Remember, you can only choose one hill.

If you die on the hill, there won't be others.

Choose carefully.

Honestly, many of the hills we make last stands on aren't worth the price.

We must decide what we're willing to shed blood over. Some epic causes and ideas are worth the blood. Others aren't.

Success, happiness, and purpose in life are linked to wise decisions on the right battles. You only have so much blood to spill.

There are only a few hills worth dying on.

Choose them carefully.

Most of the time, we should simply overlook someone's words or actions and move on.

I call it the unoffendable life.

You only have so much blood to spill. Choose on what hill to spill it.

Choose carefully *where* and *when* to make your stand.

Most fall-outs can be avoided if *one party* or the other, makes a choice that it's not worth fighting about.

Why don't you be the *party?*

However, there are times when a brave man or woman must choose to make a stand.

Climb your hill, stand astride it and make your stand.

I cannot make those distinctions for you. It's a personal decision that only you can make.

However, take some time for reflection before you climb your hill.

And when, in your heart-of hearts, you know it's right, dig in.

Just remember the rule of taking your hill: you'll often be standing alone.

Don't let that deter you when you know it's the right thing to do.

There are definite times we should dig in.

These are bleed-worthy hills.

A hill worth dying on.

I can't tell you which ones they are.

That's a very personal decision.

You can get friendly feedback, but there comes a time when a man must choose.

There are two vivid Biblical accounts of men standing their ground. Choosing their hill to die on.

Two men I admire.

One is Jesus,

The other is a follower of Jesus named Stephen.

Back in Chapter 15, "Grit," we observe Jesus "setting his face to go to Jerusalem."

He's got a bad job to do, so he sets his jaw, and moves toward his destiny.

Notice what the verse states, Now it came to pass, when the time had come for Him to be received up, that He steadfastly set His face to go to Jerusalem . . . "

His time had come.

Nobody around him knew it.

He was walking to his grave with a bloody cross on the way.

The time had come to suffer, die, and then be received up.

That served to state his resurrection awaited.

But it was tough road. *He set his face toward Jerusalem.*

A few weeks later, during what we call "Passion Week," Jesus makes another face-setting decision in Jerusalem.

This decision will seal his fate.

Jesus chooses his hill to die.

We all are familiar with Palm Sunday, and scholars agree Tuesday is the day where Jesus "Cleanses the temple."

But there's an overlooked verse in Mark 11 about Jesus' travel on Monday.

The day between his triumphal Sunday entrance into Jerusalem and his Tuesday upsetting the apple carts in the temple.

It's Monday.

Listen: "Jesus entered Jerusalem and went into the temple courts. He looked around at everything, but since it was already late, he went out to Bethany with the Twelve." —Mark 11:11.

Jesus chooses his hill five days before his death.

It's Monday, and he knows what's coming Friday.

He probably stewed in his own juices that night. Unable to sleep.

Don't forget that Jesus was fully God but also fully human.

Praying while he gritted his teeth and planned what he must do the next day.

Tuesday morning, he got up.

He'd made up his mind.

He'd had enough.

His snit was full.

I believe he was in full stride as he made the short two-mile walk from Bethany to Jerusalem.

Arriving at the Temple, he tore into the greedy merchants selling animals for sacrifice in the temple courtyard.

He was angry.

But this wasn't impulsive anger.

It was controlled anger.

He'd concluded, the day before on his Monday temple visit, that it was time to take action.

He'd chosen his hill.

He's had enough.

His anger over injustice and greed was full and ready to be poured out.

His bucket was full.

He tore into that motley crew of tradesman taking advantage of poor worshippers.

I'd like to have been there.

He began overturning tables of the moneychangers and the seats of those who sold pigeons, the sacrificial purchase of the poorest of the poor, scattering coins, tearing open stall doors.

Men running, donkeys braying, oxen kicking and snorting, lambs *baahing* as they ran for the exits.

John, an eyewitness to this, adds, "And making a whip of cords, he drove *them all* out of the temple." (John 2:15.)

I would have liked to have seen it.

I doubt if Jesus struck any of them, but I bet they scattered and ran like they thought he would.

Notice how the scripture says, "And he drove them . . . "

He wasn't after the animals. It was the scoundrels.

Then Jesus shouted, "It is written, 'My house will be called a house of prayer,' but you have made it a den of thieves."

Jesus was angry and took action.

He'd chosen his hill to die on

And that was literal. The enraged temple leaders began making active plans to kill Jesus before he could start any more mischief.

Don't miss this in Matthew 12:14: "And the blind and the lame came to him in the temple, and he healed them."

Jesus, after driving out the crooks, sat down in the temple and calmly began healing the blind and lame.

There are so many facts of this entire story that reveal Jesus, the Lord, and Savior I've chosen to follow.

One stands out.

He'd chosen his hill to die on.

And his death in five days, and his resurrection three days after that, he paid for our sins. Yours included.

There's another "Man's Kind of Man" found later in Acts 6.

A disciple named Stephen is called on the carpet by the Jewish Sanhedrin, the most powerful religious and political leaders of Israel.

After a facing a multitude of lies and mistruths about Jesus, Stephen made a decision.

He planted his feet and chose his hill to die on.

He was standing alone on that hill facing seventy of the most influential men in Israel.

One against seventy.

Stephen had chosen his hill.

He launches into a long history (the longest speech recorded in the Bible, fifty-three verses taking up nearly all of Acts 7) of God's work among the Hebrews going back to Abraham. Then he makes a blistering attack against these Jewish leaders for their rejection of Jesus as the Messiah.

Stephen had made his stand.

They immediately dragged Stephen out of the city and stoned him to death.

But he'd stood his ground.

He had literally chosen his hill to die on.

Often standing our ground is a lonely place, and often it may cost us something, but we must have some core values where we won't waver.
Choose your values and choose your hill.

The German theologian Martin Luther made such a stand. He also chose his hill.

Luther was a German theologian, priest, monk, and professor at the University at Wittenberg who began to question the policies of the Roman Catholic Church at a time when the Church's authority was absolute.

Martin Luther's speech at the Diet of Worms (also known as the "Here I Stand" Speech) is considered one of the most significant pieces of oratory in world history. It was given in response to the council's questions on whether Luther would stand by his doctrine or recant. His refusal to recant is a classic defense of personal freedom.

When the Church attempted to silence him, he stood his ground.

He was called before the Catholic council of the Diet of Worms (what a name) and told to repent.

His powerful speech at Worms ended with this bold statement, "Here I stand; I cannot do otherwise; God help me!"

His speech was central to the beginning of the movement that became the Protestant Reformation.

The echo of those words are still orbiting the earth. In many parts of the world, Followers are still saying, "Here I stand."

Don't overlook that Luther basically stood alone that day.

What's popular is not always right and what is right is not always popular.

That day, Luther risked ex-communication from the church, imprisonment, and even death.

"Here I stand. I cannot do otherwise."

There will be times when a man or woman will feel compelled to stand up and make a stand.

Compelled. I've always liked that word: "To drive or urge forcefully or irresistibly."

Something usually compels people who take a bold stand.

It's an action word.

"Here I stand. I can do no other."

I don't know how to differentiate between a picnic hill from a battle hill for you, but I believe that down in your soul, you'll know.

When that time comes, just do the right thing.

NOTES TO MY FUTURE SELF:

27

FINDING YOUR JETHRO

"Every Camp needs a Jethro."
—Red Colquitt

"Every person needs a life coach."
—Curt Iles

It's a memorable conversation with a great lesson.

In Exodus 18, Moses struggles to corral the Twelve Tribes of Israel. They've recently escaped slavery in Egypt but are now stuck in the wilderness.

Moses is trying to placate these unhappy campers.

He's overwhelmed.

Then Jethro, Moses's father-in-law, arrives. Listen to the story:
"*When Moses' father-in-law saw all that Moses was doing for the people, he asked, 'What are you really accomplishing here? Why are you trying to do all this alone... from morning till evening?' Moses replied, 'Because the people come to me to get a ruling from God. When a dispute arises, they come to me, and I am the one who settles the case...* "

"This is not good!" Moses' father-in-law exclaimed. "You're going to wear yourself out—and the people, too.

"This job is too heavy a burden for you to handle all by yourself. Now listen to me, and let me give you a word of advice, and may God be with you."

Jethro and his son-in-law Moses
Jethro arrived, saw the load his favorite son-in-law was carrying, and was dismayed.

He was an outsider, much more able to see the big picture.

He arrived from the 30,000 foot view we talked about earlier.

Jethro was a *life coach*.

He gave Moses some constructive criticism and told him why.

He even sketched out a plan in the desert sand on how to delegate and spread the load.

Jethro was an experienced and respected leader.

He had two things that elders possess: wisdom and experience.

Africans knew them as *Mzees*. Respected leader.

One of the greatest honors of my life was when the tribal leaders began calling me "Mzee."

Don't miss this: Moses listened to Jethro, acted on his counsel, and the entire horde of Hebrews ran much smoother.

Everyone was blessed, especially Moses.

He listened to suggestions to organize and delegated. That's noteworthy. Often weak leaders don't want anyone to come in and tell them the truth.

Even when told the bare truth, they often won't act on the advice.

Moses wasn't that kind of leader. He listened, took Jethro's advice, and the entire situation changed.

We all need a Jethro.

Someone with wisdom who'll come in and tell you the truth, even if you don't want to hear it.

When I first heard about Red Colquitt, I knew we needed him.

I was the young camp manager at Dry Creek Baptist Camp, and Red Colquitt was a Texas legend. He'd retired as a camp manager and now served as a consultant for Texas Camps.

One of my friends said, "You need Red come to your camp, but you'd better be ready. He'll find everything about your camp, good, bad, and otherwise."

I called him.

Red Colquitt spent a weekend observing retreats we were hosting. He carried a small notebook and took copious notes for three days.

He looked under tables, measured bunk beds and doorways, and looked into the crooks and crannies I'd forgotten to lock.

Needless to say, I was intimidated.

However, I knew we needed some solid outside counsel about how Dry Creek could improve.

At the end of the weekend, Red sat down and gave me an in-depth summary of his observations.

He was so kind in pointing out many positive things he'd noticed about our staff and facilities. Then, he went over a shopping list of things we could and should improve.

That weekend, Red Colquitt became a mentor in my life.

He became a Jethro to me and made many successive trips to Dry Creek. He had a perspective that I needed to hear.

He also became my friend.

That was the best part of the whole deal.

I believe every young person, especially leaders, needs to surround themselves with mature leaders who will listen, guide, and suggest.

We need those mentors who are willing to pour their wisdom and experience into our lives.

Throughout my life, I've been blessed to have men and women mentor me and my work.

Even as I am near seventy, I'm still being mentored. *Some of my teachers are half my age.*

Or more.

All five of our older grandchildren serve in some capacity in Creekbank Stories.

They serve as graphic artists, copy editors, social media mavens, marketing, and as general critics.

I love being with them, and yes I pay them.

They have taught me so much on technology.

"PawPaw, you mean you don't know how to do this?"

"I do now. You've taught me."

Our Jethro's may come from all directions and size.

They all have something to teach me.
You have no friends.
You have no enemies.
You only have teachers.

Here are some thoughts
Find a person *who* is already good at what *you* do.
Notice what I said, good at what you do. I've always sought out successful coaches, principals, and tough experienced missionaries.
There's a wealth of experience out there.
Find them.
Meet them.
Listen.

Surround yourself with someone who will be honest.
Who'll tell you what you need to hear, not what you want.
Be a good listener.
Notice that I *invited* Red Colquitt to visit, and made a conscious decision *to listen* and *act* on his advice.
It takes humility to take blunt advice, but we all need it.
I'm not talking about a negative person. They're a dime a dozen and can rain on anyone's parade. Find someone who will also share about what's positive.
That's called affirmation.
A wise person who closes the door, sits, and then speaks the truth.
They'll get in your face without getting in your face. They'll get in your heart where a mentor's advice can shape you.
It's called constructive criticism.
We all need it.

Remember, there is a grain of truth in every criticism.

We would all benefit from this type of life coach.

Not the kind that charges $100 per hour, but the life coach who sits in front of you at church. She's been through every season of life and has much left to give.

Just call her coach.

Or the group of grizzled Vietnam Vets who sit every morning drinking coffee at your McDonald's.

They're a wealth of information, and always *willing* to dole out advice.

Buy a cup of coffee, sit down, and listen to that bunch of old codgers.

They can be your coaching staff.

Or observe that couple who've raised productive, hard-working, spiritual children. Glean from their wisdom.

"How did you do it? What was the most difficult part? What would you do differently?

Let them coach you and your spouse.

Remember Moses and Jethro.

A leader needs a whispering encourager.

A leader needs a truth-*teller.*

Finally, everyone, leader or not, needs a high-altitude pilot. Someone who sees the 30,000-foot view.

That's called perspective.

That's who Jethro was to Reverend Moses.

They get the big picture. The goals. The purpose. Excuse the pun, but a pilot who will help you keep your feet on the ground.

Just call them coach.

"In the end, people appreciate honest criticism far more than flattery."

—Proverbs 28:23 NLT

Mentoring is about a relationship between two people.

Proverbs 27:17 states this clearly, "As iron sharpens iron, so one man sharpens another."

It's about iron sharpening iron.

However, it's hard to sharpen iron if your pocketknife is in one pocket and your whetrock is in the other. You've got to get close to someone to get sharpened.

You need a Mentor.

You must become open, transparent, vulnerable, humble, and teachable.

Sadly, those are the very reasons why many people will not seek out a mentor.

NOTES TO MY FUTURE SELF:

28

Gratitude

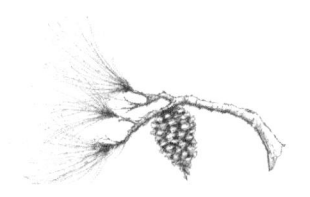

Any chapter that quotes Willie Nelson, the Apostle Paul, Jesus' brother James, Todd Strain, and Teddy Roosevelt is worth a second look.

"When I started counting my blessings, my whole life turned around."
—Willie Nelson

Gratitude is simply the act of being thankful.

It becomes a habit. The more you practice it. The more you'll see blessings for in every direction.

Just like any good habit, living with gratitude takes practice.

Like a muscle, it gets stronger with use.

Gratitude leads to this prayer of the heart:

"Lord, you've given me so much. I ask you for one more thing: a heart of gratitude."

Living Gratefully involves:

1. Being aware of the people who make our lives so rich and returning this love to them.

2. Realizing that every good gift we have comes from God and thanking Him.

3. Having such a grateful heart that it becomes easier cutting others slack.

My favorite holiday is Thanksgiving. It's the only American holiday that's not wrapped in glitzy commercialism,

Thanksgiving. We've left it alone, and it remains the designated day for gratitude.

A day to be thankful.

Remembering that Thanksgiving is not a day, but an attitude.

It is an attitude that should permeate every moment of our lives.

It's an attitude of gratitude.

Each year, I designate the month between Thanksgiving and Christmas as "Thanksgiving Month. "

It's a great season of the year to have gratitude.

"Thanksgiving should be more than a day; it should be a season."
—Todd Strain

I grew up with the old hymn,
"Count your blessings,
Name them one by one.
Count your many blessings

And see what God has done."

Yes, that could be a good project. Make a gratitude journal and daily write the things you're thankful for.

Count your blessings.

Be sure to write on both sides of the page, because you'll fill it up as you recognize the blessings all around you.

Remember Jailbird-Apostle Paul words from a Philippian prison: 'In everything, give thanks . . . " and "Every good and perfect gift comes down from the Father above."

If a man in prison can be grateful, I have no excuse.

I learned my greatest lesson about giving and gratitude in a small, dirt-floored church in a Kenyan refugee camp.

Hundreds of South Sudanese refugees crowded the building. All had lost everything, fleeing a senseless civil war.

In African culture, worshippers come forward to give their offering. A long line of women and children approached the altar. The men were off fighting in the war.

A young woman, baby on her back, came forward, knelt, and poured grain into a pot near the offering plate.

The Sudanese pastor whispered, "She has no money, so she gives a portion of her part of her grain allotment as an offering to God."

I knew that the aid agencies gave a specific amount of grain per family, and it had to last until next month.

Her grain offering touched and humbled me.

This was the picture of sacrificial giving, and I still have that moment held tightly in my heart

This was her widow's mite.

It was an act of pure gratitude that I, being from a distant planet, could not completely comprehend.

Gratitude

It's such a powerful word.

It's more than simply being thankful for one event or blessing.

It's thankfulness that flows out of the heart and examines every detail of our lives in the bright light of gratitude.

Gratitude humbles us and helps us realize that "every good and perfect gift is from above." (James 1:17)

Giving thanks to God the Father at all times and for everything in the name of our Lord Jesus Christ.

Ephesians 5:20

"Let us remember that as much has been given us,
much will be expected from us,
and that true homage comes from the heart
as well as the lips and shows itself in deeds."
-Teddy Roosevelt.

NOTES TO MY FUTURE SELF:

29

How's Your Walk?

I saw him coming and quickly ducked behind a camp cabin.

Invariably, this young pastor would find me and grasp my hand as he pulled me into my personal space. So close that I could smell the spearmint on his breath.

"Hello, Brother Curt. *How's your walk?*"

It was the middle of a hot summer with four camps behind us and four to go. It was hump week. Long days and short nights had taken a toll on me. I was running on fumes.

As we often said, "There ain't no tired like Dry Creek tired."

My energetic friend wanted to know how my walk with Jesus was.

"Brother Curt, how's your walk?"

"To be real honest, Pastor, I'm kind of limping along at the moment. It's been a long summer."

He meant well. He wrapped an arm around my shoulder and voiced a heartfelt prayer that I'd remain strong and my walk with Jesus would be fresh.

It was a sincere prayer, and I really appreciated it.

It helped.

A personal prayer always does.

Looking back, I realize it was a good question,

How's your walk?

Are you walking with Jesus?

It's such a good question that I'm passing it on to you.

So, how's your walk?

I'm not asking if you never miss Church or Mass, or if you have a spotless record on your daily Bible reading.

I'm asking, "How's your walk?"

How's your walk with Jesus?

It's a good question:

Your personal walk with Jesus.

I highly recommend Him as a walking companion. We've walked together for over fifty years and his presence still warms my heart.

There were times when I didn't think I could go on. He grasped my hand and refused to let go.

I want to walk *with* Him.

Not behind. If I drop back too far I might lose sight of him.

And definitely *not ahead.*

A man can get in some tight spots if he ventures out too far ahead.

I need to walk *beside* Him.

I want to walk *with* Him.

Yes, walking with Jesus. That's the best place to be.

By the way, how's your walk?

NOTES TO MY FUTURE SELF:

30

TAKE A KNEE

> "I'm gonna fall down on my knees,
> And praise The Lord for bringin' me peace.
> I'll lift my hands in His company
> For you know, I am grateful
> For what He has done for me."
> – "On My Knees"
> Red Clay Strays

Take a knee.
That's what coaches would say when they blew their whistle.
"All right, men. Take a knee."

Take a knee.

It's a good posture to get in.

I'm not just talking about prayer. There's much to it than that.

One purpose of taking a knee is for a quiet time of meditation.

Silent.

Alone. Shut the door.

Taking a knee is a very private time.

Don't do anything.

Just be silent.

Take it in.

Meditation gets a bad rap.

It has nothing to do with navel-gazing or Hindu mysticism.

Meditation is simply about being still and quiet. Letting the inner stillness in you silently speak.

There's no time limit on taking a knee, but I'll warn you: when you start doing it daily, your time in meditation will become longer.

It's habit-forming.

Another attribute is that taking a knee humbles you.

It's an act of submission that comes from the heart. Another thing about taking a knee is how it forces you be still.

I like how King David said this, "Be still and know that I'm God."

That's coming from a man who spent the early years of his life alone as a shepherd.

Be still.

Here's another thought: when you really get silent for a period, you'll sense God's presence.

Be still and know.

It's a private and personal thing for each man and woman.

And when you get in God's presence, don't start off babbling.

Quietly listen.

A big part of prayer is listening. Listening to that still small voice.

Yes, speak to God, Pray to God. Tell him what's on your mind, no matter what. He's a big boy and can take on anything you bring to him, He's also a Big God who works in our lives when we pray.

Although taking a knee is a good location for prayer.

But there's no requirement for the posture of prayer.

It doesn't have to be on our knees.

You can be walking,

It can be behind the wheel of your vehicle.

For years, my friend Donnie made the daily one-hour commute to the Sulphur refineries. As he drove, long before dawn, he prayed for every house along the highway from Dry Creek to Ragley.

It included our house at 3090 LA Hwy 394. My friend prayed for DeDe, our boys, and me each morning.

Your prayer closet can be in your truck cab.

Or in a deer stand.

Standing over the sink washing dishes.

It can be brief and heartfelt. During my deepest days of depression, I had two basic prayers;

"Lord, I believe. Help my unbelief."

And "Help me, Jesus. I can't make it on my own."

Looking back, those were two sincere prayers from heart.

Short and heart-felt.

And I know He heard them.

I believe God doesn't care how loud or long a prayer is. He always looks at the heart.

There's also an extreme posture mentioned throughout the Bible.
Prostrate.
Getting prone before God.
Laying your face on the floor before God.
The young people call it a "Sucking carpet."
It's the most humbling and intimate way to come into God's presence.
Getting prone hasn't been a regular occasion habit in my life.
Maybe it should be.
However, each time I've laid prone, it was in the midst of significant moment in my soul.
Often times of great distress.
Disaster. Tragedy.
But I've also fallen prone in times of great joy and thankfulness. At the moment, it felt like the only thing to do.
It's a very private thing to do.
When one of those times come, try it out.

Before we leave taking a knee and praying, I want to walk you through the steps of growing prayer.

These are best started as a child but are applicable at any season of a man's life if you need to catch up.

*Praying aloud while alone. It creates intimacy when you speak aloud. You're having a conversation with God. You're speaking out loud, but speaking from your heart.

*Not sure what to pray about? Here's a good prayer. If you're a single young person, pray for your future spouse. While you're doing that, pray that God will prepare you to be worthy of him or her when your paths finally cross. DeDe and I both prayed for each other long before we met. Praying for a future spouse spurs you on to be a better man or woman.

And when you find that soul-mate, begin the practice of praying together. It may be awkward at first, but if you can't pray together aloud, I'd step back. Chances are, one of you are going to be extremely unhappy in your relationship.

A blessing at each meal.

When your family grows, have a bedtime prayer with a precious child.

Don't wait until you think they understand, pray over that child from the moment they become part of your home. There is something magical. No, there is something miraculous in praying over a child. It changes things, including you.

Then there's the next big step: praying in a group. Praying aloud among a congregation or small group.

It's a leap, but a powerful part of your journey.

In the days of the old small Dry Creek church, men, women, and youth were often called to pray in prayer meeting with no prior warning. As I grew up, I learned to be ready just in case I was called upon. You were never too young to be called on to pray in the old Dry Creek Baptist Church. I kept the adage in mind, "No one's ever complained about a short sermon or brief prayer."

One Sunday night, when I was twelve, I was jarred fully awake with, "Curt, will you dismiss us in prayer?"

I fumbled around, but it was a benchmark in my life. The fact that one of my mentors, Ed King, had called on me to pray meant the world to me.

Praying aloud among a group scares most of us to death.

It'll be awkward at first, but it will be one more step on your spiritual growth.

---

*Finally, there's the most challenging, yet rewarding type prayer.

It's praying *with* others.

Not just, "I'll be praying for you."

It's the next step.

"Do you mind if *I pray with you right now*?"

"Right here?"

"Yep. Right here and now."

I've never been refused, and I've also never seen a person unaffected by a personal spoken prayer.

Here's an early memory on my journey of praying with another person:

Jess was Dry Creek's junk man. I'd often see him plodding along in his old truck, muffler dragging, his truck bed piled high with scrap metal.

I knew Jess through his daughter, who had been a student when I was principal. He was a single parent struggling to raise a teenage daughter.

One day, we pulled alongside each other in the post office parking lot.

As Jess and I leaned on the fence, I asked about his daughter. His face dropped and tears filled his eyes. His daughter had chosen a wayward path after high school, and they were estranged. He wasn't even sure where she was living.

His face was a mask of pain— A deep look of dejection and despair.

I felt stirred, but I hesitated. I wasn't sure how this might go with this rough-living man,

"Jess, do you mind if we pray for her right now?"

He glanced around the parking lot. "Right here?"

"Yes, Sir. Right now. I bet God can hear a prayer from a Dry Creek parking lot."

Jess nodded, "Sure."

I put my arm around his shoulder. I don't remember what I prayed, but it was brief and from my heart.

When I said, "Amen," Jess looked up

He had a look on his face that I'll never forget.

His tearful dark eyes bored into my soul.

Tears coursed down my cheeks, too.

Neither of us was ashamed.

It created an unbreakable bond between me and the junk dealer.

It was my first lesson about the power and privilege of personal prayer. It doesn't have to be in the Post Office parking lot or in the midst of a dusty African village.

It can be anywhere.

Anywhere you meet a fellow struggler.

Take the courageous step of praying with a hurting person. They're everywhere if we just take time and look around.

P.S. And don't forget to take a knee to start your day.

NOTES TO MY FUTURE SELF:

31

THE EMPTY CHAIR

The oft-asked question is "How do I learn to pray?"

The moving story below is the best illustration I've heard on prayer.

Brennan Manning is a former Catholic priest living in New Orleans. I heard him relate the following story about story from his touching book, *Abba's Child:*

Once, a woman asked me to come and pray with her father, who was dying of cancer. When I arrived, I found the man lying in bed with his head propped up on two pillows and an empty chair beside his bed.

I assumed someone had informed the old fellow of my visit, so I said, "I guess you were expecting me?"

"No, who are you?"

"I'm the new associate at your parish. When I saw the empty chair, I figured you knew I was going to show up."

"Oh yeah, the chair," said the bedridden man. "Would you mind closing the door?"

Puzzled, I shut the door.

"I've told no one this, not even my daughter," he said. "But all my life, I have never known how to pray. I abandoned any attempt at prayer," he continued, "until one day about four years ago my best friend said, 'Joe, prayer is just a simple matter of having a conversation with Jesus. My friend to told me, "Sit down in your chair, place an empty chair in front of you,

. . . and in faith, see Jesus in the chair. It's not spooky because he promised, "I'll be with you all days." Then just speak to him and listen in the same way you're doing with me right now.'

The sick man looked up, "So, Padre, I tried it, and I like it so much that I do it for a couple of hours every day.

"I'm careful, though." If my daughter saw me talking to an empty chair, she'd send me off to the funny farm."

The story deeply moved me and encouraged me in the days in my walk,

Two nights later, the daughter called. "Daddy died last night, but there was something strange. In fact, it's beyond strange—kinda weird. Apparently, just before Daddy died, he leaned over and rested his head on the chair beside his bed."

Take a knee.
Take a chair.
Get on the floor.
It may be where you find God.

Abba's Child: The Cry of the Heart for Intimate Belonging
Brennan Manning   Nav Press

NOTES TO MY FUTURE SELF:

32

IN THE WORD

"The Bible was written to be read outdoors."

—Wendell Berry

If you asked me about the essential habits I've cultivated in my life, one would be a daily time in the Word.

The Word.

That's the Bible.

As in Bible study.

Now, hear me out.

There are some simple keys to getting into the Word.

First of all, start smart with a plan.

Many readers begin with the purpose of reading through the whole Bible cover to cover. All sixty-six books, Genesis to Revelation. All in a row.

That's a goal for later.

They begin with Genesis. Lots of solid stories about who we are.

Exodus is a fascinating story of how God rescues and takes care of his people, the Hebrews.

Then they hit the vast tract of the Sahara called Leviticus. This book, part of the Word of God, speaks of the intricate rituals, laws, festivals, and traditions expected from the Hebrews.

It's tough sledding.

Honestly, I've never done an extensive journey through Leviticus, even though my son teaches Hebrew and Old Testament at a New Orleans Seminary.

I heard a speaker say, "Leviticus is inspired, but it's not inspiring."

I agree on both counts.

Would you allow me to take you on a tour on what I consider the essential parts of the Bible for a new reader?

Every book, every chapter, every word is inspired. Sooner or later, you'll be ready to walk through the entire book of the Bible.

But for now, I'd like to suggest another plan. I've returned to these books time after time in my life.

They never get old and I'm always able to mine some rough diamond from each reading.

Let's leave the desert, and jump ahead to Proverbs. Don't fret about this long leap. We'll be returning later to what we missed.

Proverbs is a wonderful common sense book written by King Solomon. It contains small adages to live by. You'll meet some of the most memorable characters in the entire Bible: the "Wise," the "Fool," the "Slanderer," the "Loose Woman", the "Proud" and my personal favorite, the "Sluggard."

Most verses are couplets contrasting the smart man from the ignoramus.

They're usually called the fool from the wise.

The Proverbs Reading Plan is simple: For example, you'll read Proverbs Chapter 20 on February 20 and find truths like,

"Wise words are more valuable than much gold and many rubies."

(Chapter 15, verse 15)

Wash, rinse, repeat.

When you reach Chapter 31, circle back to Chapter 1 on the first day of the next month.

Wash, rinse, repeat each day.

You'll never run out of wisdom and inspiration.

Because I'm a Jesus-Follower, I'm always reading in the Gospels.

I love the Gospel of Mark.

Mark is a young writer. He's getting his stories from a grizzled old fisherman named Simon Peter.

And as Mark relates that story of Jesus, he's so excited he tells it in a hurry. The word "immediately" is found thirty-five times in Mark's account. Jesus is a man on a mission, and he's moving onward toward the cross that awaits him in Jerusalem.

Because Mark is breezing along in his narrative, it is the briefest Gospel at 16 Chapters.

Next, I encourage you to invest in a deep reading of Luke 1and Luke 2.

This is the story of Jesus' life from birth to death on the cross and resurrection plus the ups and downs of the Early Church.

Dr. Luke, with the surgical insight of a physician, digs deeper into the story.

You've probably never heard of Luke Book 2.

We call it Acts.

The Acts of the Apostles.

Luke continues his two book series with Jesus' resurrection, his subsequent instructions to his disciples before ascending into heaven. The remainder of the book follows the appearance on the Holy Spirit and the early believers.

Dr. Luke tells it all. Miracles, martyrs, growth of the Early Church, demons, shipwrecks, adventuresome, travels and travails, with a snakebite thrown in for good measure.

The early part of Acts centers on Simon Peter leading the disciples and apostles as the Early Church stretches its wings to fly.

Then a major shift occurs. Acts shifts to the miraculous conversion of Saul, also known as Paul. This Christian-killer becomes a Jesus-follower and the rest of Acts, like Paul, is full of vigor and struggle.

A final word on Luke 2, I mean the Book of Acts. As you read carefully in Acts 16, Luke the narrator switches from "they" to "we."

Luke shifts from being a scribe to eyewitness! I can't imagine how excited he was to step aboard and join the story.

And what a story he tells!

Next, I'd move on to the Apostle Paul's jailbird letters.

They're called the G.E.P.C.

As in The G.E. Power Company.

These four epistles (another name for letters) are written to be passed around hand to hand, church to church.

Epistle. It's a distinctive kind of letter, one valued and worthy of honor. Not the kind of letter you'd throw in the trash can.

And two thousand years later, Paul's letters are still being passed around.

They are powerful.

Galatians

Ephesians

Philippians

Colossians

The G.E. Power Company.

They're written by Paul from different prisons to various churches he'd founded.

I'm amazed, that throughout history, some of the most powerful words ever penned came from behind prison bars.

In spite of his imprisonment, Paul writes with the big-heartedness that we love about him.

These four books had a great deal to do with me coming to a teen-age personal decision to follow Jesus.

To sum the four letters up, Paul is convinced that being a Christian is much more than an outward event. It's an explosion that happens in your heart and never get over.

Paul knew that.

Then you can loop back to Mt. Everest: the Book of Psalms.

Marching in at 150 chapters special chapters.

Most are written by David, a rugged outdoorsman who loves nature and God and is larger than life.

King David is a flawed character, a warrior, an inspirational leader, an adulterer, and a poet and songwriter. Some of his lyrics are still on the Top 100 of all time.

What a transparent man! David's story allows us to explore the heart of a great man, who like the rest of us, struggles along the journey.

One of the many reasons I believe the Bible is true is that it doesn't gloss over its heroes, prophets, priests, and kings.

David is exhibit 1 of the book telling it like it is

Now, you're on your own. You'll want to explore every nook and cranny of God's Word.

I encourage you to find a solid Bible version that connects with your heart. Go to a Bible site like Bible Gateway and look at your favorite verses in various versions.

Make use of devotions, Study Bibles, and Internet resources. Find a Bible-believing church and plug in. Find a Sunday School or Life Group to be in each Sunday.

Growing in Jesus is not a solo act. I've learned so much about the Word from others. Find a small group Bible study and continue for a lifetime. In our church, you can join in over a dozen groups that meet for one hour beginning at 6 am.

Be in the Word.

Find a like-minded group to be in.

I hope you've enjoyed our Bible tour as much as I have.

Now, you're on your own.

Get in the Word.

Onward!

NOTES FOR MY FUTURE SELF:

33

Receiving and Giving Gifts

Here's how to accept a gift.

Any type of gift. It's simple.

With gratitude.

With appreciation.

And with joy.

Don't fiddle around with, "Oh, you shouldn't have."

Or, "I bet that cost too much."

Or, the dagger-to-the-heart joy-killer, "I'm sorry, but I have one of those."

Just say, "Thank you very much."

Thank you.

Tell them how much you appreciate their gift.

"I will cherish this and place this in a place of honor . . . because it's from you."

Accept that gift with grace and a smile.

I learned so many valuable lessons living for three years among African cultures. Among the dozens of tribes we worked among were various rituals and traditions.

DeDe learned this first hand as we traveled into the Ugandan bush. Every roadside policeman drooled when they saw our whitefaces approaching in our beat-up Toyota Land Cruiser.

They'd wave us to the roadside and begin the subtle African dance of squeezing a bribe.

DeDe found a unique method to deal with these uniformed bandits. She'd bake a basketful of banana bread.

When the policeman would lean in our window to begin his interrogation, DeDe handed him a loaf of fresh-baked banana bread.

The reaction was always memorable. The speechless policeman staring at the gift in his hand.

In African, it is *baked* into their culture that you must accept every gift with grace and humility.

The policeman would stutter in an African-Accented-British-English. "This banana bread, Madame . . . you made this *yourself?*"

DeDe would smile and nod.

Mr. Policeman would regain his composure and break into a wide Ugandan smile. "Well, thank you, Madame. You are giving me a gift cooked by your hand. Thank you very very much"—

He'd hold up his loaf and wave at the armed soldiers manning the barricade. "Men, open that gate and let Madame and Mzee through."

As we hustled away, DeDe wryly said, "He wanted bread, but not the kind we gave him."

He accepted our simple gift, and it changed everything.

A loaf of bread and a beautiful African tradition.

Accept a gift with gratitude and grace.

There's another type of gift we Americans often fumble around a response for.

It's called a compliment.

We are unsure uncomfortable receiving personal praise.

Because of that, we blurt out, "Oh, it's nothing."

We wave them off. "Aw. Anybody could do it."

We should accept compliments with graciousness.

And a warm smile and sincere appreciation.

"Thank you very much. That means a great deal to me."

I've been so blessed to be a published author for twenty-five years. I don't write for good reviews, riches, or fame.

However, I'd be lying if I said I didn't treasure every kind word about my writing.

I bite my tongue off before saying, "Oh, it was nothing."

That's untrue.

In fact, it's a bald-faced lie

It took nine months of my life to publish *Where I Come From*. *Why would I say, "Oh, it was nothing?"*

However, no one wants to hear about the travails and disappointments every author struggles through at various stages of bringing a book to life. No one wants to hear that whining.

So I smile at their sincere compliment, "Thank you very much. It means the world to me that you enjoyed this book. I appreciate your kind words."

And I sincerely mean it. I'm honored and humbled when another human being is moved by words I've put on paper.

"Thank you so much for telling me."

It's the genuine gracious way of receiving any type of gift, including compliments.

Then there is the equally important act of *giving a gift*.

I'll sum it up in two words.

With Generosity and Joy.

Be generous.

Be joyful.

Be big-hearted.

Be a cheerful giver. *It truly is more blessed to give than receive.*

The joy we derive from giving a special gift is hard to describe. It truly brings inner joy.

Be generous.

I can faithfully attest to the fact that you truly cannot outgive God.

I'm not talking about about foolish giving. I'm referring to generous giving.

And it doesn't have to be money.

The gifts I cherish the most are handmade and given in a spirit of friendship. Someone has taken the time to think about a gift that touches my heart.

Those are gracious gifts. Gifts from the heart. Gifts made by hands.

On my desk, I keep a simple quarter slice of cedar. The outer bark is still rough. The cut slice reveals the beautiful wood grain that gives the red cedar its name.

On the smooth side of the cedar, my friend Kirk used a laser instrument to inscribe "Be still and know I am God."

On the base, he wrote "Kirk Cooper '24."

Words cannot express how I felt when Kirk handed it to me. It felt so personal in my hand. It was a an unique thoughtful gift made especially for me.—

He knew that Psalm 46:10, "Be still and know . . ." was a favorite verse of mine.

A handmade gift given with insight into the heart of the receiver.

You cannot beat that.

Let me sum it up:

Give generous gifts with great joy.

Receive gifts with gratitude and graciousness.

You will not go wrong either way.

NOTES TO MY FUTURE SELF:

34

INTEGRITY: DOING THE RIGHT THING

"Integrity is who you are when no one is looking,
and what you will stand up for, even if you're standing alone."
–John Maxwell

Doing the Right Thing

It's called integrity.
Integrity means doing the right thing.
Even if no one else notices or cares.

It's a matter of self-respect. I want to act in such a way that I can live with myself.

As usual, I have a story to tell.

I call it "A Honest Day's Work for a Honest Day's Work."

Dr. Charles Frusha related this story about his father, Hollis Frusha:

"One summer during college, I worked with my dad building houses. He was an expert carpenter known for doing things the right way.

"One day, we slipped up and took an extra fifteen minutes off for lunch. We worked the rest of the afternoon, and when it was quitting time, I laid my hammer down.

"Daddy said, 'No, Son. We owe these people the fifteen minutes we lost at lunch.'

"We worked those extra fifteen minutes, then shut down and went to the house.

"I learned something from that day. Do the right thing even if no one else will know. Have integrity."

I call Mr. Hollis's example, "An honest day's work for an honest work's pay."

Whether you're in the mill, classroom, or sawing 2 x 4's, it's a maxim to live by.

An honest day's work for an honest day's pay

A man or woman of integrity will refuse to coast.

They won't get lazy and "just mail it in."

A man or woman of integrity will always take their work seriously.

Our work comes in various sizes and colors.

My first job was picking up paper at Dry Creek Baptist Camp. I was thirteen and rode my bike daily to work. I tried to do my job right and took pride in keeping the Campground clean.

Even a teen can show integrity by their work effort.

Little did I know that twenty years later, I'd become manager of Dry Creek Camp...

and still be walking around picking up paper.

Solomon said in Ecclesiastes,
"Whatever your hand finds to do, do it with all your might."

I call it the Pineywoods Work Ethic.

If it's worth doing, it's worth doing right, especially if it's for God, and when it comes down to it, everything we do is for God.

In my small hamlet, we believe in working. Many of my friends work in various aspects of the timber industry. We call it, "Working in the woods."

Beauregard Parish is basically one large forest dotted with small farms and communities. Forestry moves our Parish, which has the motto, "Money grows on trees."

Work is important and reveals our integrity, regardless if it's cruising a tract of timber or in the corner office.

It's the Pineywoods way.

Truthfulness

A large part of integrity is being honest. Being a man or woman of your word.

Just tell the truth.

A Thomas Jefferson quote sums up the slippery slope of lying:

He who permits himself to tell a lie often finds it much easier to do it a second and third time, till at length, it becomes habitual; he tells lies without attending to it and truths without the world believing him. This falsehood of the tongue leads to that of the heart and, in time, depraves all its good dispositions.

You can avoid this slippery slope by always telling the truth. Being honest.

Telling the truth is a habit just as much as habitual lying.

To maintain integrity, I must be truthful.

Because losing one's integrity is a slow, often overlooked download journey.

Cutting corners.

Not being truthful.

Hidden moral lapses.

And once lost, integrity is difficult, if not impossible, to regain.

"I believe that it is better to tell the truth than to lie. I believe that it is better to be free than to be a slave. And I believe that it is better to know than to be ignorant."

— H. L. Mencken

Integrity may mean standing alone because what's right isn't always popular, and what's popular isn't always right.

"The one thing that doesn't abide by majority rule is a person's conscience."
—Atticus Finch, *To Kill a Mockingbird*,

Speaking of the Pineywoods, I have another story about integrity and doing do the right thing.

It's a story about not cutting corners.

I learned it as I walked my grandsons through a special plot of ground called Dry Creek Cemetery.

We walked past the graves of generations of my people to the SW corner of the cemetery, where a grave was being dug.

THE THREE TREES

Noah and Jude stared down into the yawning hole. It was their first glimpse into an open grave. It's a pretty sobering sight.

The head gravedigger, Kevin Kingan, walked over to my grandsons. He used a shovel to carefully square off a corner of the grave. "Boys, it takes me about thirty extra minutes to do it right, but I put in the extra time. It's worth it."

He tamped down the red clay around the concrete vault. "I just pretend it's my mother's grave, and that helps me do it right."

I wondered if I my grandsons would remember this lesson.

I haven't.

Thanks, Kevin, for your lesson. I'm honored to pass your story on to readers around the world.

I spent the first fifty years of my life with what the world would deem simple people: pulpwood haulers, single moms, meat cutters, dairymen, carpenters, loggers, and gravediggers.

These hard-working blue-collar workers had so much to teach me as a young man.

The value of an honest day's work. The pride of a job done well.

A reminder that digging a grave is not just a job, but an act of love toward a family of strangers.

Integrity.

Doing the right thing.

Honesty.

Make it a life habit. Do it right.

That's integrity.

"Whatever you do, work at it with all of your heart, as working for the Lord, not for men."
Colossians 3: 23-25

Proverbs 18:9
"The one who is truly lazy in his work is brother to a vandal."

Postscript:

Young people don't appreciate graves and cemeteries. After an earlier trip, one grandson announced, "Don't go off down to Dry Creek with PawPaw. You'll spend the whole day looking at dead people."

NOTES TO MY FUTURE SELF:

35

KINDNESS

> "There are three ways to ultimate success:
> The first way is to be kind.
> The second way is to be kind.
> The third way is to be kind."
> —Fred Rogers, aka Mister Rogers

Always be kinder than necessary.

It's a trait that both blesses the receiver and the giver. It leaves both with a spring in their step.

All of my life, I've been the recipient of so much grace and kindness. The old Dry Creek I where I grew up was awash with kindness.

It wasn't a perfect place, but folks, especially the older ones, always showed me kindness.

I'm sure it was partly due to my family's deep roots in the community. Clayton and Mary Iles's son was always treated kindly. In a rural community where we called almost every older person uncle and aunt, I received extraordinary kindness from these folks.

As I began branching out from Dry Creek, I still encountered kindness, often in unexpected places. I learned that those with the least worldly goods frequently showed the most kindness to others.

I noticed the compassion of others. Compassion is when kindness puts on its working clothes.

Compassion is kindness in action.

The Good Samaritan "had compassion on him" and took action.

Compassion includes empathy.

The ability to put yourself in someone's shoes and share their pain. To feel for someone.

Hurricanes Katrina and Rita in 2005 unleashed compassion throughout my state.

The storms brought out the best and worst in my home state of Louisiana. I came to believe that disasters and tragedy don't create character, but rather reveal it.

What is inside a person comes pouring out just like the water that rushed through the 16th Street Canal levee breach in New Orleans.

Dry Creek Baptist Camp, where I served as manager, became a hurricane shelter for a revolving door of about three hundred evacuees in the weeks after Katrina. They came from all walks of life, each with a unique sad story of how they ended up in our rural Pineywoods community.

Our surrounding area responded to this invasion, not with resistance but with kindness. I'll never forget a precious couple who had recently lost a teenage son, counting out thirty-one hundred-dollar bills and saying, "You use this to help these people and do it in memory of Ethan."

I had no words to say, and even now, I am moved recalling this event.

When sister Hurricane Rita hit us squarely in late September, I saw amazing kindliness among my neighbors. Everyone got up from the storm, brushed off, and went to work helping each other.

Genuine kindness costs something. It is given freely but costs the giver time and money, and it may be inconvenient. However, it is such a freeing event.

However, it seems natural to be kind to neighbors.

Kindness to strangers is what most amazes me. I saw it after Katrina, then later after Rita, when I stood in a Red Cross food line receiving a hot meal cooked by fellow Baptists who'd come to our aid in SW Louisiana.

Our three-year sojourn in Africa opened my eyes to this kindness to strangers.

Once again, DeDe and I saw the best and worst in people. We were thrust into a civil war in South Sudan and saw the ignorance of tribalism and greed.

At the same time, we saw such kindness. Nowhere was this more evident than along the borders of South Sudan and Uganda where thousands of refugees had fled.

I asked a Ugandan why they so quickly opened their hearts to these strangers from alien tribes. He smiled. "Baba, we've all been refugees ourselves at one time or another. How could we not return the kindness shown to us in the past?"

I saw this kindness shown in hundreds of unique ways. Most were simple but life-changing. Most involved sacrifice on the part of the giver. Africans have few material possessions, but I never ceased to wonder about those who had so little giving what they had.

It was kindness personified.

A final word on kindness.

It is not a weakness.

The world will often scoff at proffered kindness as naïve.

Kindness is always a long-term investment.

I believe kindness is one of life's greatest assets. It's an investment that, as you give it away, only grows inside you.

Always be kind.

And always be kinder than necessary.

Kindness: a language the blind can see, and the deaf can hear.

-Unknown

"Be ye kind one to another."

-Paul in Ephesians 4:32

NOTES TO MY FUTURE SELF:

36

Encouragement

"Encouragement is something that doesn't cost anything to give, yet the outcome is priceless"
—May Hill

Everyone needs it.
Encouragement.
If there's anything I've learned, it's that folks need encouragement.
Not just some.
All.
Everyone you and I encounter is carrying some kind of burden.
Some burdens are obvious, while others carry unseen burdens. Those can be just as heavy, maybe even more so.

You and I can encourage them.

They need hope.

Courage.

Inspiration.

As I've mentioned throughout *The Three Trees*, this life statement has guided my life:

"Be a man God can use, be an encourager, and be respected by those who know me best."

I'm called to be an *encourager*.

It's not my job. It's my calling.

My life, my writing, and my words are about encouragement.

I am humbled by the platform God has provided and given me as a writer.

In today's amazing digital world, the written and spoken word can travel into nooks and crannies throughout the earth.

This revelation has helped me focus more on what my written (and spoken) words are about: to encourage my fellow journeymen on our shared life road.

This world throws a great deal of discouragement at all of us. Like you, I need a spoonful of good news.

There's plenty of wet rags typing away. (Have you ever heard of two things called "X" and "Facebook?")

I have instead chosen to be a good news reporter. An encourager.

I'm not naïve. I've lived in and among war zones and famine in refugee camps. I've seen the evidence of man's inhumanity to man.

It's not my job to major on the meanness in this world. Even amid heartbreak and turmoil, I'm called to be an encourager.

I could talk more about encouragement. Instead, I'll do what I do (and love) best. I'll tell a story.

There is still disagreement about how, and even if, this event occurred.

It's a story too good not to tell.

The 1936 Berlin Olympics are among the most famous Olympiads of the 20th century.

Its location was Germany.

Its time was Europe was building toward another war, less than twenty years since the last Great War.

There wouldn't be another Olympics until after the coming worst war in history ended.

Then, there was the setting: Hitler wanted to use the backdrop of this event to showcase his Nazi party and the country of Germany.

An exhibition of the Third Reich and its Master Race.

As the Olympics unfolded, the most famous athlete of the Berlin Games was a Black American named Jesse Owens. He won four gold medals and captured the attention of the World.

But our story is about what happened in the long jump semifinals. It was still known as the broad jump in 1936.

Jesse Owens had fouled on his first two attempts at the jump. His approach steps were off, causing him to overstep the foul line at the beginning of the jump pit.

As a frustrated Jesse Owens pondered his final attempt, a fellow competitor approached him.

His name was Luz Long, a German long jumper. Long talked to Owens about adjusting his steps and jump-off point to avoid fouling again.

Using this information, Jesse Owens made a clean final jump and advanced to the finals, where he won the gold medal.

Luz Long finished second, winning the silver medal. His advice to Owens likely cost him Gold. However, he never expressed regret about helping his fellow competitor.

Jesse Owens remains one of the most famous Olympians of all time.

Luz Long is largely unknown. He later died in 1943, fighting for the Wehrmacht in Italy during World War II.

But nearly ninety years after his act of encouragement, Luz Long lives on in this story.

Encouragement. It's something all of us can do.

It's something all of us should practice daily.

Encouragement.

It's a good word.

Postscript on the aftermath of the Berlin long jump finals.

"Luz Long won the silver for second place and was the first to congratulate Jesse Owens. They posed together for photos and walked arm-in-arm to the dressing room.

Owens said, "It took a lot of courage for him to befriend me in front of Hitler. I would melt down all the medals and cups I have and they wouldn't be a plating on the twenty-four karat friendship that I felt for Luz Long at that moment."

—From ESPN documentary, "Jessie Owens Returns to Berlin."

NOTES TO MY FUTURE SELF:

37

STEWARDSHIP

30.63141 degrees N
93.06108 degrees W
Coordinates: Clayton Iles Pond
Dry Creek, Louisiana

I don't think there's a better place to talk about stewardship than the levee of our pond.

That original pond washed out a generation ago. and DeDe I put in a wildlife pond.

That's what it's become.

A wildlife pond.

A wildlife pond named after my Dad, Clayton Iles.

Clayton Iles Pond.

Canadian geese pay their daily visit from a nearby pond. Like clockwork, A lone egret glides in each evening.

Purple martins, who love being near water, twitter and swirl overhead with their happy sone.

A pair of squealing wood ducks glide into the wooded north end with a splash.

It's important to remember how this pond and the surrounding land were *handed down* to DeDe and me.

We're the fifth generation owners of this family land. From the day it was homesteaded in about 1890, no one has paid one red cent for this acreage that we *now call ours*.

My great-great grandparents, John and Sarah Wagnon, homesteaded 120 acres and built the log house that still stands.

When the Wagnons died in the 1930's, the homestead was passed on to their two daughters, Louise, and Dosia.

Louise was a schoolteacher who never married. After her death, my great grandmother "Dosia" Wagnon Iles Inherited the entire 120 acre tract and the Old House.

Dosia and her husband Frank Iles only had only one son, my grandfather Lloyd Iles.

It's very unusual for third generational land to only have only one heir with undivided property.

Stay with me. We'll return to this wildlife pond soon.

You've got to understand this plot of land before you understand pond built on it.

About 1960, Dosia donated the east forty acres of the one hundred twenty acres to her grandson, my father Clayton Iles.

My Daddy's gift of forty acres left the remaining eighty acres the Old House.

It's still a family joke as to if Daddy asked for it or his grandmother chose to give it. He was the oldest grandchild and the favorite.

I suspect he "discreetly hinted" for it and she gladly gave it.

Even his siblings laughed about it. My Uncle Bill said, "Heck, there's no way any of us wanted it. Who wanted to live out there in the middle of nowhere?"

But Daddy wanted to move to Dry Creek and raise *his family* on *family land.*

We lived in the Old House until he built a house in 1960.

My Mom was a real trooper. The Old House had no indoor plumbing, one water tap, and a tub for bathing. There was no insulation and you could peer through floor cracks to see dirt.

It was a Mecca for mice, chicken snakes, spiders, and roaches.

I once asked her how Daddy got her to move to Dry Creek.

"It took four years of nagging."

Dad built our house, and he and Mom made that simple wood frame house their home.

THE THREE TREES

It's the house I grew up in—135 long strides—from one porch to the other. It's where my sisters and I grew up and where my mother still lives.

About twenty years before his death, Daddy, being a land man, divided his undivided forty acres ways between him and Mom's house, my two sisters, and me.

My two sisters and Mom still live on their respective plots of land at the end of Clayton Iles Road.

DeDe and I never built on our land.

I said that there were enough crazy Iles's down that road already. It would have not been wise to add another.

DeDe and I raised our family near the heart of Dry Creek Community five miles away.

Close enough, but not too close.

But my heart never veered far from our homestead and the Old House.

Daddy gave DeDe and I a long rectangular twelve acres on the south side of the forty acres.

Even though we don't reside on it doesn't mean I don't cherish our strip of land.

It's part of the land that was homesteaded by John and Sarah Wagnon, who passed it onto their daughter Dosia Iles, and she gave part of it to my Daddy.

I'm the fifth generation to be a caretaker of this land.

Although my roots go so deep in that sandy soil, I don't own it.

I'm the current steward.

That's stewardship.

That's where the pond comes in.

It was originally dug by my Dad.

During the 80s, the levee washed out and it sat empty until about 2018.

Our family had a new wildlife pond built.

The levee is on my past of the acreage, but much of the northern end falls on my two sister's land.

We don't know where "each part" of the pond is.

We don't know, and I don't care to know.

That's why we named it Clayton Iles after our father. He was given the land by his ancestors and it now belongs to his descendants.

I'm ashamed to admit that for a recent time I began to think of it as "My Pond."

I learned a humbling and painful lesson last year that I will not repeat again.

I was reminded that it was our family's pond, not mine.

It's not my pond. It is *our* pond.

Owned by the descendants of Clayton and Mary Iles.

It's dusk and I sit by myself beside a camp fire near the pond levee.

Our pond AKA Clayton Iles Pond.

As the dark deepens, I take a last glance at the land on each side of the pond, which serves as a demarcation point between our two native soils.

The soil to the east of the pond is sandy and loamy and well-drained. It's perfect for growing pines and watermelons.

It's where we planted rows of young longleaf seedlings. They're tall enough now that the evening breeze whispers through them.

The wind in the pines. It's a sound that always draws me in and soothes my soul.

Our land west of the pond slopes down toward Crooked Bayou Swamp where the soil becomes wet and boggy. Pines don't grow well here and the land becomes the domain of the oaks, beeches, and hickories.

My cur dog Bandit peeks up as I speak, "My pond. Our pines. Our family land. What a joke."

I pet his head. "Bandit, I don't own this anymore than you do."

He flops his tail against the ground and smiles. Don't tell me dogs don't smile. You just haven't owned one that did.

"Boy, I'm just a caretaker of this spot of land I'm currently sitting on."

I'm a steward. A caretaker.

It's temporary.

Stewardship involves humility. We realize we don't really own it.

We don't own it, but are responsible for it

There's a delicate balance there. Ownership and Stewardship.

As I've said before, I don't know if I own this land or it owns me.

Once again, the levee coordinates are roughly 30.63141 degrees N 93.06108 degrees W

Come on by and walk the levee.

It *"don't belong to me"* anyway.

⚜

For me, stewardship is much more than my land and Clayton Iles Pond.

It's also about all of the material possessions DeDe I have been given.

Yes, that includes our finances.

I have several creeds about money:

I've been blessed.

God owns it all.

I try to live open-handed and open-hearted.

I've tried, but you cannot out-give God.

⚜

I've also a steward of time.

I want to value the precious time I have. I want to use this time to pour into the buckets of the people and things I love.

That's why DeDe and I moved to the city. We moved to Alexandria to pour into the buckets of our grandchildren.

As an older man, I realize I'm a steward of my entire family.

I am the leader of this extended family.

A Clan.

A Tribe.

I want to be faithful.

A faithful steward in every area of my life, including being the current caretaker of one part of a wildlife pond south of Dry Creek, Louisiana.

Starting at Southwest (SW) Corner of the NW Quarter of the SW Quarter (NW/4 of SW/4) of Section Eleven (11) Township Five (Five) South, Range Seven 7 (Seven) West, Beauregard Parish Parish, State of Louisiana, containing 11.9 acres, more or less, along with all improvements thereon.
 - SW corner of Sidney and DeAnise Iles property, Dry Creek, Louisiana.

NOTES TO MY FUTURE SELF:

38

The 30,000 Foot View

I'm always amazed at how different Louisiana looks from an airliner cruising at 30,000 feet.

I'm flying from Houston to Orlando, and everything seems so small from that altitude.

I strain out my window to find a landmark as we cross the Sabine River into the western Louisiana's No-Man's-land. I'm reminded that my home parishes of Beauregard, Vernon, and Sabine are one vast pine forest dotted by small towns and farms.

We fly east leaving the Pineywoods and pass over the flat Cajun Prairie and its neat squares of rice fields.

East of Lafayette, we enter the vast Atchafalaya Basin Floodway, the largest freshwater swamp in America.

THE THREE TREES 199

Soon we near the Mississippi, "The Father of Waters." We follow along the path of the river until we near New Orleans.

From the 30,000 foot view, it is clear: this large city is surrounded by water on every side.

. I trace the Mississippi.

I pick out the white Superdome as we speed over the city center. Tracing the Mississippi's curved course through New Orleans, I understand about the river's features here.

When I standing on the French Quarter levee, I'm always confused about the direction of the river's current toward the Gulf. Is it flowing toward the big bend to my left or toward the big bridge on my right.

It's because of the unusual feature where the Mississippi makes a sharp U-shaped crescent. That's why New Orleans is called The Crescent City.

Below the city of New Orleans, the Mississippi River resumes its southern journey to the Gulf of Mexico. Excuse me, the Gulf of America.

I can easily discern the river's path from my seat six miles high.

I call it the 30,000-foot view.

Every young person and leader needs to have a 30,000-foot life retreat.

It's a *periodic planned period* to step away from the fray and see the big picture.

It takes *discipline* to take a break when there's so much to do, but it's essential to stay on course.

To keep the main thing as the main thing, and to see from a different angle.

It must be away from the home and office. You need a distraction-free place to think and plan.

I carry a large sketchbook. I call it my 30,000-foot view book. It's where I sketch out the big ideas and book outlines for the coming year.

I use a pencil. Some mistakes in life can be erased, just like erasing a mistake on paper.

I need a review day. A 30,000 foot view day.

It doesn't have to be an entire day. Then again, you may need to escape to a hideout for several days.

It can be as simple as a foggy morning spent shivering in a deer stand. Amazingly, worries and indecision melt away and you can see the way forward clearly in the most unusual places.

There's one thing that is essential to a productive review.

Turning off your screens.

Ouch.

I make my living on screens. My phone, laptop, and iPad are my creative connections to the world.

However, on a true retreat, I cut the cord to my screens.

That's why I take my journal and sketchpad.

Whether it's one hour.

One day.

Or heaven forbid, one week.

Because we're addicted to our screens, it is difficult to unplug and shut down.

You're not indispensable. Believe it or not, the world, including your world, can operate without your presence for this period of time.

Yes, you should have a way where a close family can contact you. There are ways to stay connected to the key people in your life while cutting off notifications to the outside world.

You cannot have a true retreat with constant beeping. Notifications don't mix with seclusion and solitude.

It's a time and place to step away.

It's called a retreat. It's a military word. An essential word for the lifelong learner.

Retreat.

Slip away.

A retreat involves stepping away from your normal life and hectic work schedule.

Notice the action verb.

Step away.

You must *move* physically, emotionally, and spiritually to have a true retreat.

You can find that place of solitude when you discover your personal hide-out.

To a quieter place.

Just do it.

A review is also a great time to look back.

A review builds balance into your life, and it keeps you from coasting, or

burning out.

We regain our perspective, focus, and passion.

It's harder to coast when you regain those three.

A retreat is a chance to look back. I often take previous journals and examine what's been going on in my life.

A review.

But a retreat is much more than looking back.

It also provides a focused view of what is most important in the coming days, months, and even years.

To get your inner compass out and set a heading for your true *priority*. That compass can show where you've come from, but its most important task is the way ahead.

You notice I said *priority*.

Priority.

It's singular. The *thing* that matters most of all.

A list of objectives or goals is good, but they're not your Priority

Your Priority, which we will discuss later is often called a Life Statement, is the idea burning in your heart, keeping you dreaming during the night.

It's where you state what you believe and how it encompasses your reason to exist.

That sounds pretty serious.

Because it is.

But we'll help you in the next chapter of *The Three Trees* begin crafting your personal life statement.

That one Priority that makes you tick.

🌲

There'll be dozens, even hundreds, of connected strings to your priority.

They're all important, but not your priority. It's normal to call them priorities as long as you remember you can only have one priority.

The best use of a 30,000 foot retreat is to write a personal life plan combined with a life statement.

It's called your life plan, and it will be as individual and unique as you are.

Your life plan. We'll explore a blueprint in the next chapter.

It'll be a fun journey. Personal growth is a discipline but can be enjoyable project.

I won't write your life plan and statement for you, but I'll be looking over your shoulder encouraging you on the journey.

By writing a life plan, you'll do what 98.87% of people never do: you'll have a written plan to guide your life.

But to write an effective life plan, you've got to see the big picture.

That's why having a 30,000 foot view is so important.

Go for it. Let's fly!

As I am prone to do, I close with a story. I learned about the necessity of retreating during a wonderful but hectic phase of my life.

Here's how I recorded it in my journal:

Banda Island
Lake Victoria, Uganda
Equator
May 11, 2014

Everyone needs a place to go for a 30,000 foot view.
A hideout.
A secluded place of retreat.

My African cloud-level review was on Banda Island, a small secluded island in the middle of Lake Victoria.

During our time in the bush, people constantly surrounded us. Many asking for money for school fees, teeming refugee camps where the tribes throng around wanting to know when the UN Food would arrive. Others pressed around to touch a "Mzungu" (White Man) for the first time.

It was such a joy sitting huddled around a campfire shoulder-to-shoulder with a group fellow believers singing, worshipping, and eating roasted crickets late into the night. DeDe and I were each holding a baby, neither one wearing a diaper. I called them "ticking time bombs."

It was simply wonderful.

It was memorable.

And it was completely exhausting.

Exhausting.

Physically. Spiritually. Emotionally, and Mentally.

After about two weeks in the Bush, we'd return to our Ugandan home in Entebbe near the Airport.

Whipped.

It was a time to rest, glean from our notes, and catch our breath.

While at home, I loved walking the streets of Entebbe. There is nothing like the sights, sounds, and bustle of an African town.

However, my walks weren't restful.

Every vendor wanted to see me sell me a $10 Rolex knockoff watch, miracle home-brewed medications, or animals and produce of every kind.

There were mothers requesting money for school fees. Others begging for help with medical expenses. They besieged me at every turn.

I returned from my walks drained.

We loved our home but it was never quiet. Two disco bars, a Muslim mosque, and a Hindu temple surrounded us.

I had to find a hideout.

A place away from, and above, the din.

I found my 30,000 foot getaway on a tiny sand-covered spit of land called Banda Island. With DeDe's permission, I'd catch a fishing boat going to Banda Island, a small island in Lake Victoria.

It was always a trip to remember. Children in blue uniforms laughed and sang as they returned home for school holidays. An older Ugandan woman grinned, holding five chickens tied together by their feet, while two goats roamed freely in the hold. The fishy smell of buckets of flopping live tilapia permeated the boat.

It was unforgetful.

My retreat had already begun.

A weight lifted from my shoulders, and peace settled over my soul as land faded behind us. After a thirty-minute ride, the boat would run aground and I'd heft my pack and wade knee deep to land. I'd rent a small open-faced cabin and enjoy being alone and the peace that comes from solitude.

I used the time to ponder, review, pray, and plan for our upcoming excursions.

Honestly, much of the time I did nothing.

Catching up on my sleep and watching the amazing spectacle of a sunset or listening to the surf on this large lake.

This was my 30,000 foot view retreat.

I returned to land refreshed, with new plans sketched out and ready to go.

Back here in America, I don't have Banda Island, but I've got an assortment of similar hideouts.

Susan Toth Allen described her personal hideout. "A closed door, a comfortable chair, a view out a window. Maybe that's all a hideout needs."

You need a hideout.

In fact, you need several hideouts.

Your review doesn't have to be a few days on a sandy island.

Vary the lengths of your reviews. They can vary from an early morning coffee hour on the patio, a quiet day hidden in the library, or three days in a secluded at our Old House log cabin.

These are all 30,000 foot retreats.

To be honest, you must *fight* to build these times into your life and schedule.

Then you must be *brutal* enough to protect them.

And *disciplined* enough to take them.

Take that 30,000 foot retreat, and if you need to, toss that iPhone overboard into Lake Victoria.

You can pick it up on the way back.

NOTES TO MY FUTURE SELF:

39

A LIFE PLAN

I want to be a man God can use,
I wish to be an encourager,
and I want to be respected by those who know me best.

It's time take to take stock.

It's important to know where you're going. It's sometimes called your inner compass.

Your compass points in a certain direction. Hopefully, becoming the person you were meant to be.

I call my inner compass "My Life Plan."

I'll share each part of my life plan:

A Life Statement to live by. It's a simple way to show what really matters.

A Life Verse to steer my heart and mind.

A list of words that sum up what I'm about. I call mine, *"Ten Words to Live By."*

Then I draw what I call my *Concentric Circles*. These are the people who are most important to me. To keep me squared away, I have a list of the levels of relationships in my life. Stay tuned for Chapter 40. I'll share from my heart how the circles ground me on the relationships in my life.

Additionally, I have what I call *buckets*. These are the people and things I want to pour my life into. I only have a limited amount of "water" so I choose to pour carefully.

I'll also share about the qualities and pursuits I'm pouring myself into. Life is too important and precious to be poured into leaky buckets.

One page contains the buckets of the people in my life that I love the most.

I call them my Clan.

They're my inner circle.

The closest members of my family.

You'll meet them and their buckets in Chapter 41.

In addition to the *people* who matter most, a Life Plan should contain the *things* you value most.

A Life Plan is a work in progress.

It is never finished, and it shouldn't be.

If you're growing, your Life Plan will be, too.

Looking back, my Life Plans for 2005 and 2015 are different from 2025.

My core values haven't changed, but how I list them has.

Notice I used the word *list*.

A Life Plan must be written, and it must be placed in *places* where you see it daily.

Emmitt Smith, former running back for the Dallas Cowboys, said, "If it's in your head, it's only a dream, but when you write it down, it becomes a goal."

Write it down.

Write on your palm, scribble it on paper, or on your iPhone.

Here's the best idea: get a journal and begin taking notes of your life.

Your hopes, dream, goals, disappointments, and the stories you notice when you glance around and listen and look.

Above all, jot it down.

Once again, put your life plan and life statement everywhere you spend any time.

I'm a member of Calvary Baptist Church, a large church in Alexandria.

I've learned something invaluable. Calvary isn't a big church. It's a large church made up of dozens of multiple small groups meeting under one roof. I'm a part of five different "little churches" at Calvary.

Calvary has developed a simple life statement:

"We are striving to become biblically rooted believers, deeply connected friends, missions minded servants, and faithful disciple makers."

Four simple goals.

Biblically-rooted believers.

Deeply-connected friends,

Missions-minded servants.

Faithful disciple-makers.

Calavary's life statement is posted everywhere.

Seldom does a service pass where some church leader doesn't state this mission from the stage.

We've heard it some much that most members can recite it.

It's the Mission Statement of who we are, and more importantly, who we are becoming.

It's planned, posted, and proclaimed.

I call it the inner compass of our church. Keeping our large ship on course.

That's the difference between a dream and a vison.

It's written and exposed.

Then put it out there where everyone can see it.

I wouldn't be surprised if Calvary didn't get TP printed with it. Don't laugh. I bet you can find it on Amazon.

A personal life statement is similar to what a business or church does.

Yours is better. It's yours. It is personal.

Write it down.

Keep improving it.

Put it everywhere you can see.

THE THREE TREES

When you've written it out, it's been vocalized.

You can begin developing your personal life statement during the morning quiet time you've carved out.

But above all, write it down. That's the difference between dreamers with their heads versus the achievers with their feet on the ground.

I've known families who have developed a family life statement with input ranging from a four-year-old to adult family members.

That's sound like a great project. Make it clear what we're about, what we'll do, and even what we, as a family, will not do.

There's no bad place to place or write it

We talked earlier in Chapter 4 about the art of journaling.
Journaling and having a life statement/life plan go hand-in-hand.
All of my life planning is handwritten.
Write it out.

Here's more about my personal life statement and the life plan surrounding it.

Years ago, I began patching together a life statement.
Many organizations call it their mission statement.

My life-statement makes up the beating heart of what I call my life plan.

Over most of my adult, life my life-statement has varied little, consisting of three brief statements,

I want to be a man God can use.
I wish to be an encourager,
and I want to be respected by those who know me best.

They're simple and memorable.
Long life statements normally end up lining waste cans.
Keep it brief.
My three short sentences serve as my daily inner compass.
They serve as an honest mirror of who I am and who I'm becoming.
I'd like to touch upon each one.

🍂

BEING AN USEFUL MAN

First, If I'm going to be a God-useful man, there are certain things I won't do; and just as importantly, there are things I'm compelled to do.

I can measure every decision in my life by asking this question, *Will this make me more useful to God, or will it harm or disqualify my usefulness to God's work?*

ENCOURAGEMENT

I'm not sure if encouragement is a spiritual gift, but it's a word that describes part of who I am.

I talked about encouragement in Chapter 36.

It's the *keyword* in my life. I strive to be an encourager.

Encouragement is more than a word.

It's an word in action.

Encouragement compels me to take action.

It results in a deep empathy for others who are hurting or discouraged.

God put an encouraging spirit within me.

It's how I try to live.

It's how I write. I'm an encouragement-inspirational writer.

Yes, there's plenty of bad stuff out there. I'm not naïve. I worked amongst a civil war and refugee crisis in African. I've seen the worst in people, and I've seen evil up close.

I only know my assignment.

I'm called to be a good news reporter.

My writing and speaking platform statement is "Sharing moving stories that encourage and inspire."

I want to encourage others in every encounter in my life.

RESPECTED

Finally, I want to be respected.

Respected by those who know me best.

My *Clan*.

My wife DeDe, our three sons and their precious wives, and our nine precious grandchildren. Thankfully, my clan includes my 90-year-old mother. Very few men my age have a living mother.

These are the inner concentric circles of my life.

If these people respect me, nothing else matters.

I don't get my self-esteem from a best-selling book, award, or public acclaim.

If the people who know me best respect me in spite of my flaws, everything else is secondary.

These are the three parts of my life statement.

I view it my life statement daily in the flyleaf of my journal.

My life statement isn't original. I borrowed it from a speaker. He laughed. "I borrowed it, too. Use it."

There's no copyright on my life statement either.

You're welcome to take it and tweak it, but I think it's most important that you conceive your own rock-solid life statement.

You can use it too as part of your starter kit.

Once again these are the three steps in my life statement.

I want to be a man God can use.

I want to an encourager.

I want to be respected by those who know me best.

Go out and write your own.

It's personal.

Don't feel that you have to get it perfect the first time. That's what the blank sketchpad and pencil eraser are for.

Dream.

Think big.

But above all, write your own personal soul-clinging life statement that fits perfectly within your heart.

MY LIFE VERSE

I believe in having a life verse to live by.

My lifelong favorite verse has remained unchanged since adulthood.

It comes from the words of Jesus during His Sermon on the Mount: "Seek ye first the Kingdom of God and his righteousness, and all these things shall be added unto you."

—Jesus in Matthew 6:33

This verse has guided me, given me focus, and revealed the amazing truth that you cannot outgive God.

I glance at it daily and hold it in my heart.

Choose your own verse and place it in various places where you'll encounter it daily.

Because it's from God's Word, it will change and direct you.
Try it.

MY TEN WORDS

In my life plan, I also list ten words I've chosen to live by.
They compose the things that really matter.
I keep this list of my *Ten Words* words in my Life Plan.
These words make up the DNA of my life.
Adherence to these words has helped me become the man I'm trying to live by.
Here are my current Ten Words:
Perseverance
Encouragement
Reach: Influence/Impact
LLL Lifelong Learner
Legacy
Kindness
Passion
Stewardship
Humility
Integrity

They form the fabric of my life.
The Ten Words serve as the qualities I desire in my life,

JUST SAY NO

The last part of my life plan deals with the art of saying "No."

Most of my life plan is focused in the things that really matter, and how to make them a part of my daily walk,

However, a few years ago I began thinking of the art of saying "No."

I was being asked to do too much. Most requests were valid requests, and involved good things, but overwhelmed and took me away from my family.

"Join this."

"Attend this."

"You cannot afford to miss this."

"We need you to do this."

The list never ends.

I realized I couldn't say yes to everything entering my life.

Just say no.

Saying no. It's a difficult art to master.

I once read of a successful businessman who had a sign on his desk, *"I am most proud of the things I've said no to."*

It's much easier to answer "Yes" to every commitment or request.

But sometimes we need to say "No" to less important things so we can say "Yes" to what truly matters.

It may be the long-held Saturday morning golf game versus seeing your kid whiff three times in a T-ball game.

He'll remember your presence long after you've forgotten your golf handicap.

Remember that every yes or no decision is a trade-off.

Yes and No always means something is taken and something else is left behind.

They're called trade-offs.

It's the path of least resistance to simply say yes to everything.

We become squeamish at saying the word "No."

Why not dress it up with an honest smile? "That sounds like a wonderful project, but at this time I'll pass."

I have a list of automatic No's in my life. I call them "My Irrevocable No's."

They are very personal but i felt I should list them.

I always start with this pertinent question.

"Now, why in the world would I want to go and do something that stupid?"

Here they are:
* I will not be unfaithful. I will not cheat on my sweet wife, DeDe.
*I will not take money that doesn't belong to me.
*I will not lie.
*I will not intentionally hurt anyone. If I do, I'll try to make it right.
*I will not be unkind.
*I will not talk ill of anyone behind their back. If there is a problem, I'll address it promptly, personally, and face-to-face.
*I will not coast.

There you have you have it: the intricate parts that make up a good Life Plan.

A brief life statement.

A life verse.

Words to live by,

And the automatic "No's" guard you from temporary lesser things of life.

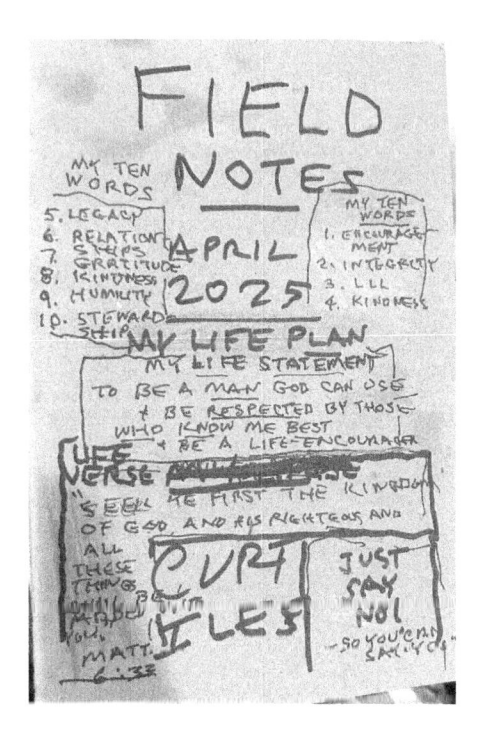

The front page from my April 2025 Journal.

An effective Life Plan should be posted in various places where it can take root in your heart.

I purposely used this rough page as a reminder that your plan doesn't have to be on a placard or desk sign.

A Life Plan is always a rough draft and constantly evolving.

Your life plan will, and should, be different from mine.

But by all means, get that pencil or pen out and begin your personal plan.

You'll never regret it.

NOTES TO FUTURE SELF:

40

CIRCLES

MY CONCENTRIC CIRCLES OF LIFE
INTERNET FRIENDS
GOOD FRIENDS
LIFETIME FRIENDS
MY BIG FAMILY
MY CLAN
DEDE
MY WALK WITH JESUS

CURT ILES

"He who defends everything defends nothing."
—Frederick the Great

> A hundred years from now it will not matter what my bank account was, the sort of house I lived in, or the kind of car I drove... but the world may be different because I was important in the life of a child.
> —Forest E. Witcraft

Let's face it.

We cannot be everything to everybody.

Because I'm an avid friend-maker and friend-keeper, I'm blessed with so many friends. I never realized the doors of friendship writing would open.

I am a man most blessed.

However, I must choose which relationships I will hold closest to my vest and heart.

That is the purpose of my concentric circles.

I love and appreciate everyone in each circle above, many of whom I will never meet personally.

I cannot sacrifice my inner circle, for other relationships or preoccupations.

My circles keep me focused on the things that really matter.

I check myself against them daily.

MY WALK WITH JESUS

That's my most important personal relationship in my life.

If I keep my walk straight and close, everything else will fall in place.

DE DE

Of all of my human relationships, my wife is the priority.

We've been life partners for over forty-five years.

She deserves all of my time, love, and attention.

I love all of my other family members, but DeDe is who most has my heart.

MY CLAN

Jesus' inner circle were called disciples.

I call my closest inner circle "My Clan."

Clan.

It's a powerful Scot-Irish word.

"A clan is a group of people united by actual or perceived kinship and descent."

Most Pineywoods people trace their lineage back to Scotland and Ireland.

Most of my clan are blood-related.

Others are like family, and I view them in the care of my Clan.

My key clan group are the eighteen members of the Curt and DeDe Iles clan.

Our clan started with two of us on August 9, 1979.

I'm astounded that the clan DeDe and I oversee now number eighteen.

Our three sons and their sweet wives.

Our precious nine grandchildren.

And my one-of-a kind mother, Mary Iles.

I'm responsible for them.

They're the primary recipients of the water in my bucket.

I choose to pour myself into the buckets of those in my clan.

During my daily and weekly reviews, I look over each of their labeled over each name and pray for them.

I also use this bucket page to ensure I'm actively pouring into their lives. They range from age five to eighteen, so I've got to be creative how I pour into their lives.

What am I pouring?
Time.
Love.
Energy.
Fun.
Stories.

MY BIG FAMILY

I group my Big Family as my extended kin plus special relationships. I'm blessed with a fine extended family and a host of wonderful friends.

LIFETIME FRIENDS

I highly value my lifetime friends. We may not see each other often, but I still feel a kinship.

Some are the type of friend that even though we've been apart, we immediately pick up from our last visit.

"Even though our hands may not often touch; Our hearts always do."

When we moved to Alexandria ten years ago, I knew practically no one. It's been a joy to form new relationships.

But nothing can replace those lifetime friends. Our bond stretches back decades and I highly value them.

I feel a kinship with them.

GOOD FRIENDS

As you move to each of my circles, the personal relationships change.

I love my good friends but the depth of these relationships vary.

I'm not in constant contact with all of them.

INTERNET FRIENDS

Many friends I know through the internet.

They're important even though our hands don't touch and probably never will.

God has blessed my writing ministry. I've been privileged to have friends I would never have known without the tools of the digital age.

Draw out your concentric circles.

The headings and names in your circle will differ from mine.

However, write them out.

Name them.

Place people in their respective circles.

It's a powerful reminder of keeping the main thing the main things.

Make sure you're pouring your life into those inner circles.

NOTES TO MY FUTURE SELF:

41

BUCKETS

I've never known a man who died regretting time spent with his family.

B uckets are symbolic of the relationships in your life.
    As a young science teacher and coach, I posted the following in my classroom:

"Hey, I don't care how much you know until I know who much you care."

It's anonymous but remains in my heart.
You must care about people to reach them.
That's called empathy and that's what the buckets are about.
Your life bucket should be full of love and care.

Buckets.
You're carrying one.
And so am I —as is everyone else.
Our respective buckets aren't filled with water.
What we are carrying is much more precious than water.
These buckets contain your life.
Let's call them life-buckets.
You may choose to call them love-buckets.
There are many items in your life bucket.
Love.
Time.
Faithfulness.
Empathy.
Those are only a good starting point.
You can add your own.
These life buckets contain your legacy.
I'm not referring to what you leave behind when you die.

Legacy is about what you're doing today to pour into the buckets surrounding you.

This is not about the proverbial "Bucket List" of what you do before you die.

Those types of bucket lists are fine. I love any "to-do-list" stating things we want to do in the future.

Your Life Buckets are about what you're doing today.

Life-Buckets are about today and where you've chosen to pour into.

Pouring.

That's an action verb.

As in "I'm pouring."

I'm referring to buckets that have their foundation in the heart and care about the people and things around them that matter most.

In my life plan sketchbook, I draw a series of buckets. I draw them by hand. I enjoy the act of drawing buckets, circles, and boxes in my sketchbook. It makes it all seem more personal.

I draw an assortment of buckets on the page.

The buckets on my sketchbook's right circle are the most important buckets in my life.

People.

Relationships.

Remember: everything rise and fall on relationships.

Speaking of relations, the right page of my sketchbook is filled with the people I care deepest about.

They're clearly labeled, those closest to me with a sharpie (literally and figuratively.)

Some are smaller buckets, but I especially make sure to keep them full.

You met many of these people in the previous chapter on "Circles."

I call this inner circle by many names.

My close family.

My tribe

My clan.

They are my people.

Those people of my inner circle of part of my life statement, "Be a man who is respected by those who know me best."

That's a tall order.

You have yours, too.

Write them down and give proper attention to each one.

NOTES TO MY FUTURE SELF:

42

BEWARE OF LEAKY BUCKETS

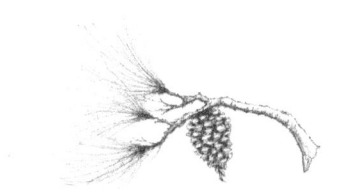

A Word of Warning

I hate to follow a positive chapter with warnings.

But there are some essential truths about your life.

You only have one bucket.

No one else can carry your bucket for you. i.e. if you set it down, it will stay exactly where you left it.

It'll be awaiting your return.

If you ever return.

The saddest things I've ever seen are men or women who've lost their bucket.

They've misplaced their life-bucket.

The saddest sentence in the English language, "He lost his way."

We shake our head. "She got off the path and lost her way."

That's a bad place to be.

There's an equally worrisome thought:

Failing to replenish your bucket.

It's called going dry.

It's a sad state to be in.

Dry. A dusty bucket.

During the depths of my depressions, my bucket was dry.

I had no tears.

I had no outward emotions.

With time and the love of a strong woman, my bucket slowly refilled.

I had the blessings of gifted healing doctors and life-changing medications.

So I'll take my meds until the day I die. If a medicine can help me stay upright and out of the dark, I'll gladly take it.

I want a full bucket.

Remember, you have a limited amount of water in your bucket. There are limits on diminishing water.

How to replenish your bucket?

We mentioned several of them in Chapter 38, "The 30,000 Foot View."

Getaways.

Hideouts.

Take these periodic breaks.

Jesus took time to step away. If he made time, so should you.

Be careful where you're pouring.

Every pour is a tradeoff. Wherever you pour means someone or something else will be neglected.

That's okay if we have our buckets lined up in priority order.

It's also easy to pour ourselves into leaky buckets.

Things that don't last, or rusty buckets. You don't want to pour your buckets into things that should be avoided.

Be careful where you're pouring.

You only have so much water.

There are many good buckets out there, but you cannot fill them all.,

And remember that every cupful you pour into one bucket means others will get less.

Yes, pour your all your life bucket into a variety of things: work, career, hobbies, sports, or even church.

Don't sacrifice the best for the good.

Choose buckets that really matter.

Those that hold water.

NOTES TO MY FUTURE SELF:

43

WHY I WRITE... AND WHY YOU SHOULD, TOO

WHY I WRITE

It was Saturday afternoon when I received the man's call.

"Sir. I just got out of Angola. God changed my life while reading your book. I promised myself I'd contact you when I got out."

I didn't get *his name.*

I don't know how he found *my name.*

How did my book find its way into Angola Prison?

But it did, and his call gave me a great gift that I still carry like a candle in my heart.

Twenty-five years of rejection letters, deep bouts of depressions, and days when I didn't know if I could make it. Stretches when the darkness sapped my creative energies.

Yet, I still heard his soft voice like a flickering candle.

"Angola . . . your book . . . God used it . . . changed my life."

The Three Trees. Where will this book you're holding go?

I hope it first lingers in your heart.

I pray it impacts and encourages you. Who knows where it will go next? Feel free to keep it and re-read it over the years.

But you have permission to pass it on if you're finished with it. Share it with a friend . . . or send it to Goodwill.

Who knows where it'll end up?

Like the winged pine seeds that flutter down from pinecones, our words—written or spoken—can travel on the wind far beyond the place of their birth.

That's what I want my books and stories to do.

Travel far and wide to places I'll never go.

I can share stories globally from the Old House Porch in the red rocker my great grandfather, Frank Iles, sat in.

Today, there is no limit where a book, blog, or podcast can travel.

I always place a new book in God's hands.

Many times as I press the Amazon "Publish Your Book" button, I lift my hands as if releasing a bird.

Travel.

Travel far.

Far and wide.

"Oh, the places you'll go."

-Dr. Seuss

WHAT I WRITE

I wish for my writing to have a deep-rooted reverberation in the hearts of readers. I write about what I know: the unique and fascinating stories of Louisiana's people, places, culture, and history.

I write stories that move me.

I write memorable books and stories that I'm comfortable with my grandchildren reading.

I humbly work to be a good steward of this privilege.

I worship when I write, and I write when I worship.

In summary, I write because it's who I am.

I am a proud Southern writer and a curious historian. I'm a storyteller.

It's my calling.

It's my mission.

As John Wesley said,

> "Do *all* the good you can,
> In all the ways you can,
> In all the places you can,
> At all the times you can,
> To all the people you can,
> As long as ever you can."

I believe Wesley was referring to the ripple effect we can all have.

The ripples, which like the pine seeds, can travel far.

Yes, that's why I what I write and why I write.

WHY I WROTE THE THREE TREES

Because I had something I wished to say.

I had a manifesto.

"A manifesto is a written declaration of the views of an individual which often goes against the status quo."

The Three Trees is a manifesto. It's my Manifesto.

My Pineywoods Manifesto.

These are my field notes.

I wanted to vocalize my life beliefs.

I just feel better getting it off my chest.

That's where a book starts.

Not in the brain, but first in the heart.

Let me be clear. I don't think everyone should write a book, but I believe everyone should seriously contemplate about it.

When are you going to write your book?

Or better yet, when are you gonna tell your stories?

And who are you gonna tell them to?

And what medium or tool will you use to *vocalize* your life-story?

"Vocalize" simply means you're going to speak your story out loud.

It may be on paper, a laptop, or aloud.

That's not a simple task. It's risky.

There's a quote, "Most men go to their graves with their *songs* still in them."

I believe it's much more prevalent that men and women go to their grave with their *stories* still in.

That's sadder. Most of us are not musicians and would never produce a song, but all of us are storytellers.

And those tales, whether large or small, need to be passed on.

Vocalize your life.

Get out there and write that book that's been swirling in your mind for years.

I never remember my MaMa Pearl Iles being a writer. She was too busy cooking and reading Harlequin romances.

But in her later life, after a stroke had robbed her of her speech, she wrote her life story in a tablet.

Before she died, she silently handed it to her son, my Uncle Bill.

He typed it and kept it as family treasure.

It was the story of her two lives.

A girlhood growing up in the rice fields near Oberlin during the Great Depression. Thoughts on growing up as an English-speaker amidst a rich French culture.

She vividly tells my favorite story of the night her Uncle Quincy, a recent Angola Prison escapee, showed up in the night in need of a change of clothes and some cash.

Then her life changes dramatically when, as a teenager, she married Lloyd Iles and moved into a new life in Dry Creek at what she called the Old House. Four generations of the Iles clan smothered her in love.

She never left.

But she left behind a written account of her life journey.

It was a memoir, not an autobiography.

Thank goodness, memoirs, whether short or expansive, have much more of an authentic, honest voice.

I plan to is publish a book from her written record. It'll be on Amazon with a unique ISBN number with a physical copy housed in the Library of Congress.

No one outside our family may buy it, except Debra Tyler who has already made a pre-order.

That's not why I'm publishing it. MaMa Pearl had a story worth telling.

She silently vocalized her life.

She wrote it down in her own words in a simple rural style.

In writing, we call it voice.

It's the unique way a person writes.

Your voice.

Put your voice on paper.

With the help of the Lord, I'm going to *re-vocalize* Pearl Iles's memoirs.

I want to share her wisdom, faith, and love of life with the world.

The world? Don't you think you're overreaching?

I've learned Amazon can travel anywhere.

And the Internet is forever.

Who knows what a simple 20th Century woman might have to say to the 21st Century?

Or beyond.
As we say,
See Dirt?
Throw seeds.

Do you have that compelling story within you?

Write it down and put it out there.

It's so easy for an author to become paralyzed. You feel that It's too risky to put it out there for anyone to see, even if it's your kid sister.

Get it out.

Don't wait to get it perfect.

> "If I waited for perfection, I'd never write a word."
> —Margaret Atwood

However, don't apologize if you choose to keep your writing close to the vest.

Or close to your family.

Write and tell your stories for your children and grandchildren.

You'll give them an immeasurable gift

Unforgettable.

It may be several generations before a family member digs it out and discovers it is a treasure.

Regardless, tell your story, and it will encourage them to pass your stories on to the next generation while adding their own.

That's legacy at its best.

Remember the three trees. Pass it on.

Tell your story.

No one can tell it better than you.

NOTES TO MY FUTURE SELF:

"

44

BURNED YET BLESSED

As we near the end of *The Three Trees*, I'd like to share the amazing story of the lifecycle of Louisiana longleaf pines.

It's a story about resilience.

I walk through my stand of longleaf pines. A hot woods fire has burned through them, leaving only charred stick-like trunks, all straw burned off.

The intense fire consumed smaller trees and charred the bark of larger trees to over ten feet. It's a sad sight to see acres of pines with blackened trunks and brown straw.

Looking across the tract along the Reeves highway, I see pines of all sizes blackened and charred. The fire burned the needles off the smaller trees, leaving a pitiful stump. If I didn't know better, I'd say this entire stand will need to be replanted.

But there is a fantastic story behind the fire and longleaf pines. Understanding the history of the longleaf pine, *Pinus palustris,* is crucial to grasping this story. This native tree, also called the yellow pine, ruled the virgin forests of the South from Virginia to East Texas. Because of its hardiness, adaptability, and ability to grow in shallow, sandy soils, it covered much of the acreage of the southern United States.

These beautiful pines existed in vast tracts called pine savannahs. These upland areas contained pines scattered throughout grassy areas. Because of the tall grasses, fire was always a reality during the dead of winter, when frost had killed the surrounding vegetation.

Before humans lived in the Pineywoods, lightning strikes would spark fires that might burn for days a waterway or rain extinguished them.

The first people to burn the woods were the First Americans. We called them Indians, but they were really the First Americans.

They burned the savannahs to see game animals better and lessen the chance of their enemies hiding nearby.

White settlers burned the grasslands to improve grazing land and eliminate pests.

No matter the reason for these fires, the longleaf pines continued to grow. Wildfire easily kills non-native pines like slash and loblolly, yet fire seems to help longleaf pines thrive.

Looking at the charred trees, I'm reminded of how longleaf pines need fire to thrive.

Longleaf pine grows much slower than the other pine species. Because of that reason, most replanting of pines has favored the faster-growing species, such as loblolly or slash pines.

The early stage of a longleaf pine is called the grassy stage. It has a minimal trunk above ground, and the long green needles more nearly resemble a wild type of grass than a tree. The pine will remain in this "long straw" stage until a fire sweeps through.

During this stage, the tree will remain dormant in growth due to what is called brown spot needle blight. This fungus attacks the top growth area of the young pine, called the candle bulb.

The combination of the tall grass competing for sunshine and nutrients and the needle blight keeps the young pine tree from growing. The surrounding grass keeps the area moist, which is the condition the needle blight needs to attack the small pine's topmost candle bulb.

Consequently, the longleaf sapling will remain indefinitely in this grassy stage—alive, yet never growing upward.

A longleaf pine will never reach its potential until a fire rushes through, killing the grass and other trees vying with it for water, sunlight, and nutrients.

The needle blight succumbs to the fire's heat. Now the bushy longleaf pine is freed by the fire to grow to its intended height and size.

And doesn't a longleaf grow tall and beautiful! Their resilience is one of the many reasons I love this species.

In the succeeding weeks, I inspect the field to see any new growth. Finally, in March, the tops of the trees show new green growth. A healthy candle bulb, some a foot long, reaches upwards.

Over the coming weeks and months, this candle bulb turns into a tree trunk and sprouts fresh pine straw, and this once dwarfed longleaf pine will never again have to compete with the grass for water, sunlight, or food.

Knowing about this species, I also understand that this same growth is taking place underground. If you've ever seen the exposed tap root of a longleaf pine, you know it has a deep, strong foundation for growth.

There is a spiritual application to the story. We all experience being in the fire at various times in our lives. None of us are exempt. Your fire will probably be much different from mine.

Regardless, God wants to use this fire to shape you and use you. Throughout history, the people God has used the most have been those who have worked through challenging circumstances to grow to their "maximum" height for him to use.

Are you in the fire? If so, remember that God has not abandoned you. Just as Shadrach and his two partners were joined by God in the Babylonian fire, you are not alone. And you can rest assured that your faithful Father is using this fiery trial to shape you and use you as never before.

And remember that these same pines have been burned by the hot fire. They burn them yearly for continued maximum growth.

Looking at them, I hope you recall the story of how these longleaf pines have been burned, yet blessed, by the fire.

I close with a precious letter from a special friend. Her name was Joy.

What a fine name.

Joy Tanner

She wrote, *"2005 was a tumultuous year of storms for Jack and me; the fiery fatal plane crash in which our daughter lost her life; the people with whom we spent twenty years in Cameron Parish who lost it all because of Hurricane Rita; the news that our deceased daughter's only child is going to Iraq; my husband Jack's Lou Gehrig's disease.*

In spite of the significant losses, we've become better instead of bitter. It's a peace that comes from the inside, from inside the heart, where the mold cannot grow.

And the water cannot flood.

And the hurricane-force winds cannot reach.

And the flames of the plane crash cannot burn up.

Amen and amen."

Joy Tanner

Burned, not broken.

Burned, but better.

Joy's letter reveals a brave and tough woman who has not allowed her spirit to become hard.

Her name—Joy—says it all.

Joy—unlike happiness—comes from inside and cannot be taken away by situations, storms, or even tragedies.

Despite being hammered repeatedly in 2005, Joy Tanner emerged from the experience better, not bitter.

Burned yet blessed.

May the same be said of each of us.

NOTES TO MY FUTURE SELF:

45

KEEP YOUR FEET ON THE GROUND

> "It's like gravity's gone,
> And I'm just floating'"
> —"Gravity's Gone"
> Drive By Truckers

I always admire successful men who've kept their feet on the ground.

Who've never forgotten their core values or where they came from. They're not floating.

They have a strong gravitational pull that has kept their feet on the ground.

That's what I like best about my friend Wayne.

THE THREE TREES

He's one of the most unique men I've known.

He's a creative artist. He doesn't paint on a traditional easel.

His easel is a computer screen. Through his sharp vision, he can produce stunning graphic art.

He is creative, and he's eccentric.

That describes me, too.

Being called eccentric and unique are badges we creative artists proudly wear.

I'm also creative and hyper-eccentric and, like Wayne, I'm not afraid to get off the beaten path.

I think we're both happy being off the four-lane super-highway of normal life.

Perhaps our heart connection is because of that.

Wayne is unique.

Unusual.

Innovative.

He marches to the beat of his own drum.

Wayne's distant drumbeat has led to outstanding success in his business and his personal life.

And through all of this, he's kept his feet on the ground.

He founded Ugly Mug Marketing, a premier marketing agency in Central Louisiana. Despite great success in his business, Wayne has kept his Priority and priorities in order.

You see, success either makes a man better or destroys him.

I've watched plenty of both.

I've watched Wayne grow as a man. He is one of the hardest working, innovative leaders I've known.

But what I like about Wayne best is how he's kept his priorities in order, especially with his family and faith.

I admire how he cares for his wife, Heather, and their children.

My favorite thing is how he takes one of his children to lunch weekly.,

It's a small matter, yet it's a big thing.

Ask one of his children.

As we've become friends, I've realized he is a man of deep faith and deep convictions, quiet but consistent in his faith and walk with the Lord.

Wayne is a man of integrity.

He is a servant-leader to his staff.

In essence, despite his success, he's kept his feet on the ground.

In the parlance of Dry Creek, he's not been "clay-rooted."

It's a verb in our culture.

He's not been *clay-rooted*.

He's not been knocked off his feet by either the success or challenges of life.

🌲

Here's a lesson from our sad time of storms in Louisiana.

The Louisiana hurricanes destroyed thousands of trees.

This sad scene unfolded in two ways.

The tall pines, with their deep taproots, broke off like matchsticks. However, others survived because of their ability to sway with the wind.

The heavy, shallow-rooted hardwoods fell, showing their extensive root systems.

These oaks and their cousins had been *clay-rooted*.

It's a verb in our culture.

"Clay-rooted."

Such as, "They got in a fistfight and that bigger boy *clay-rooted* him."

Or, "That defensive end *clay-rooted* the lineman before he tackled the quarterback."

In both instances, a force knocked them off their feet.

They'd being clay-rooted.

The man with his feet firmly on the ground is not likely to be clay-rooted.

Yep, he's got his feet on the ground.

And that's a good thing.

It's the mark of a successful man or woman who've not left their values, morals, and family behind.

They've not floated off or up with their success.

I asked Wayne for some tips he'd recommended for staying grounded as a leader.

> 1. Mirror Leadership: don't hold others to a standard you're not willing to hold yourself to

2. One way: my way isn't "the" way; it is only "one" way

3. Servant Leadership: a true leader has no one "under" them. A true leader knows their role is to serve those on their team.

4. Curiosity: when furious, get curious

Those are of the words of a grounded man who's kept his feet on solid ground,

In spite of the storms of life, he hasn't been clay-rooted.

And I don't expect he'll ever be.

> "But whose delight is in the law of the Lord,
> and who meditates on his law day and night.
> That person is like a tree planted by streams of water,
> which yields its fruit in season
> and whose leaf does not wither—
> whatever they do prospers."
> Psalms 1:2-3

Observing Wayne, I think of Thoreau's words,

"If a man does not keep pace with his companions, perhaps it is because he hears a different drummer. Let him step to the music which he hears, however measured or far away."

March on!

> "Go for your dreams with great intensity."
> —Don Gray to his son John circa 1996

NOTES FOR MY FUTURE SELF:

46

A Vista with "Noodle" and "Pilgrim"

Before leaving *The Three Trees*, let's return to a higher altitude.

It's called a vista.

It's not 30,000 feet high. Instead, it's 5269 feet above sea level atop Mt. Katahdin in Maine.

It's a clear day atop Maine's highest mountain. Clear enough to get a panoramic view.

It's a vista.

You can turn in any direction and see for miles.

A panorama.

This is where I want you to meet two fellow climbers named Noodle and Pilgrim.

Katahdin is the northern terminus of the Appalachian Trail that begins (or ends) in Springer Mountain, Georgia: 2,189 miles south.

I've scrabbled, huffed, and climbed to reach its summit, and the view is magnificent. Maine is a state of thousands of lakes and our vista makes each appear like scattered glass across the landscape.

In every direction, I could only see forests and lakes.

The climb was worth the view, or is it "The view was worth the climb."

Either way, it was breathtaking.

The view was a vista.

What made standing atop Katahdin memorable was my climbing partners.

Their trail names were "Noodle" and "Pilgrim."

They were thru-hikers. They'd walked every step from Georgia to reach this summit.

I stood apart from them, realizing this was a sacred moment for them.

It was the culmination of their separate dreams.

But it exceeded a mere dream. They'd put hiking boots to the ground and made it here.

Very few thru-hikers who begin in Georgia make it to Katahdin.

But Noodle and Pilgrim had.

When they walked past me, I asked, "Was it worth it?"

Noodle said, "Every single mile was worth it."

PIlgrim added, "And I loved every miserable step."

Before they walked away, I asked,

"How you'd get here?

Pilgrim laughed. "I saw a white blaze on a tree in Georgia and followed the markers until I reached here."

Noodle pondered, then said, "Perseverance. So many days I wanted to quit, but I didn't. I hefted my pack and trudged north through muddy bogs and steep rocky climbs."

Yes, it was simply perseverance.

I left them soaking it in their dream.

I wondered how it felt to fulfill a life-time dream.

But wait, I *know* how it *feels*.

My life journey is comparable to Noodle and Pilgrim's.

I got here one step at a time.

The experts claim it takes five million steps to traverse the two-thousand miles from Georgia to Maine.

Noodle and Pilgrim did it, one step at a time.

I'm nearing seventy and I've got here by following a lifetime of markers.

One step at a time. One white blaze at a time.

And I can attest that the vista I'm standing on is worth it all.

I hope *The Three Trees* has been your trail guide on *your* journey.

I'm honored and humbled that you've taken the time to follow all forty-eight chapter-blazes in this book.

I leave you with one word.

Perseverance!

NOTES TO MY FUTURE SELF:

47

Finishing Strong

"Finish your food. Don't squander the opportunity. Don't just get to the championship. Win it."
—Lebron James to A.J. Brown before Super Bowl 2025

1968 Olympics
Mexico City, Mexico

It's a story worth retelling.

His name was John Stephen Akhwari, and he had the dubious honor of finishing last in the Marathon at the 1968 Mexico City Olympics.

John Stephen, a Tanzanian runner, finished more than one hour after the winner had circled the track at the Olympic Stadium.

Most of the crowd had left, and the sun had set when John Stephen limped into the stadium for his last lap. He was the 57th runner and the last to run the entire 26.2-mile race.

There's more to his story than finishing last. During the race, John Stephen took a nasty fall, injuring both his knees and shoulder. Despite this, he ran on.

When he reached the stadium, the sparse crowd, recognizing his determination to finish, cheered him on as he finished the race.

Afterward, he told a reporter, "My country didn't send me five thousand miles to start the race. They sent me five thousand miles to finish it."

Thanks, John Stephen, for a lesson in perseverance and commitment.

You finished your race.

Your placement doesn't diminish the fact that you finished. And you finished strong.

Finishing is such a wonderful word.

We find the same dedication in the Bible's description of good King Hezekiah, the king of Judah:

"For he held fast to the Lord . . . "

Holding fast to the Lord.

Not giving up.

Finishing the race.

Finishing Strong

"Life should not be a journey to the grave with the intention of arriving safely in a pretty and well-preserved body, but rather to skid in broadside in a cloud of smoke, thoroughly used up, totally worn out, and loudly proclaiming "Wow! What a Ride!"
—Hunter Thompson

It may seem counterintuitive to close a chapter on finishing strong with an admonition to leave behind some unfinished work.

But it needs saying. *Leave behind some unfinished work.*

My dad's younger brother, Bill Iles, is one of my heroes. Uncle Bill has been one of my greatest encouragers and mentors.

He is arguably Southwest Louisiana's most renowned living artist.

Even at age eighty, he still paints every day. His studio features several works in various revisions.

I remind him that God has given him three gifts at eighty: a steady hand, good eyesight, and a sound mind.

He was born to paint.

Somewhere in his vast collection is one of his earliest teenage works. It's watercolor on a rough sheet of plywood. It depicts a pioneer on the plains returning to his wagon with a pheasant in hand. He used the knothole in the plywood as part of the painting.

He's never stopped painting.

He never will.

And that's why he'll leave some unfinished work on his easels when it dies.

It's okay to leave unfinished artwork behind.

It's the sign of a man who used God's gift to him: he painted every day.

I understand about unfinished work.

Like Uncle Bill, I'm an artist.

My brush is a pencil, and my canvas is my journal and laptop.

I practice my art every day.

I write.

I write something daily.

A writer is someone who wrote today.

When my life ends, I'll definitely leave some unfinished work behind.

Some half-written novels. Outlines of stories and books in my journals or in my mind.

I have entire folders entitled "Future Books" and "Story Ideas."

I won't get around to them all.

That's okay. If I'm writing every day, there'll be loose threads hanging.

Unwritten stories, books, and words I've left behind don't bother me.

It doesn't matter if someone finishes them or not.

That won't be my problem.

My assignment is to write every day, following my writing creed, "Sharing moving stories that encourage and inspire readers."

Sharing.

Moving stories.

Encouragement and inspiration.

To my friends and readers.

That's my calling.

A writer is someone who wrote today, and a committed writer will leave some unfinished work behind.

I'd better get busy. I don't mind leaving unfinished work behind, but I'd better get back to work.

The less I leave behind the better.

I have some books burning a hole in my heart.

I need to be writing.

A writer is someone who wrote today.

"Hi Yo, Silver away."

NOTES TO MY FUTURE SELF:

48

Epilogue: A Log Older Than Louisiana

Log sill under The Old House, Dry Creek, Louisiana

You've noticed that I write about things that last.

I'm curious about items and values that stand the test of time.

Things that have been through the storms of life and emerged unchanged.

There's nothing wrong with temporal and transient things. We are all surrounded by a plethora of plastic, wire, metal, and paper that enrich our lives.

However, I'm most interested in the things have been tested by time and are still rock solid.

That's why I've always loved the big sill log under the Old House.

The floor of a log cabin rests on a long horizontal log called a sill.

Most log houses have three long parallel sill logs for the house to rest on.

Our Old House has a two sill construction.

The east sill has always attracted me. It's larger and rounder than its fraternal twin sister.

The tree rings are clearer.

I've never been able to pass it without stopping.

As a kid, I'd walk by and give it a good swift kick, testing it.

It didn't move an inch, and I only stubbed my toe, so I stopped that foolishness. Also, I had a better upbringing about how to treat my elders.

As a young man, my connection with the old log continued.

I'd take a knee and tap on it.

It was as solid as the day in 1890 when newlyweds John and Sarah Wagnon built the house they'd live and die in.

I thought about the difficulty of felling a large tree with a crosscut saw, trimming the limbs, and rolling or hauling to its resting place.

I run my hand over its rough texture. I'm reminded that despite the fluctuating stock market and cost of eggs, some things remain unchanged.

The back cover of "The Three Trees" features the Old House log sill.

If you read the back cover copy, it states that this book is about relationships.

It's about things that last.

THE THREE TREES

Solid things.

Time-tested.

Because when it's all said and done, it's about relationships.

Because I love our rich Louisiana history, I'll weave an underlying thread about that log sill holding up the Old House.

The average lifetime of a present-day longleaf pine is from 100 to 150 years. The virgin longleaf of the Pineywoods may have lived longer.

Counting the rings on the Old House log sill shows that it was about 100 years old when felled in 1890.

So it's possible this longleaf was a sapling blowing in the wind when the ownership of this land bounced back and forth between Spain and France.

Then France and Spanish.

And then America and Spain.

During these decades, the region became a disputed territory. The fifty-mile-wide swatch between the Sabine and Calcasieu Rivers became a *Neutral Territory,* or by its more common name, "The Neutral Strip."

My people knew it as "No Man's Land" and "The Outlaw Strip."

Regardless of the name of this region, this special longleaf pine continued its upward growth.

Our pine grew on the fringe where the virgin pines and Crooked Bayou Swamp met.

Growing despite who claimed the land beneath it.

It knew its job. Grow tall and straight, dropping large pine cones to seed the area.

Then things changed in 1803 when the United States purchased a vast region of North America from France in the 1803 Louisiana Purchase.

It was still growing when Louisiana became a state in 1812.

The area became part of the Territory of Orleans, owned by the United States.

However, the disputed strip continued to be a point of contention between the Americans and the Spanish in Texas. The disagreement between the nations persisted until 1821, when a treaty signing granted the strip to the United States.

Then the Neutral Territory officially joined the State of Louisiana. And is to this day.

More or less. We've still got a streak of not liking to be told what to do.

It comprised a part of St. Landry Parish, a large administrative district.

In 1840, Calcasieu Parish was carved out of St. Landry. Because of its size, which covered most of the heel of the Louisiana boot, it became known as Imperial Calcasieu Parish.

During the only full-scale war in North American history, the Civil War, our tree didn't take sides.

It just kept growing.

Just before the turn of the century, the Wagnon family homesteaded 120 acres along Crooked Bayou.

They built the Old House on the fringe where the virgin pine hills end and descend into Crooked Bayou Swamp.

About 1890 is when my ancestors felled the big pine.

1890. Its active growing life then.

That was a long time ago.

Benjamin Harrison was president.

Louisiana was one of forty-four states in the Union.

The big longleaf lay on the ground, but its useful life continued. They placed the log as part of the foundation of the log cabin.

It became one of the foundations of our family.

And it still is.

Louise and Theodosia, the young daughters of John and Sarah Wagnon, moved in and brought life to the new home.

I can imagine them scampering along that big log before it was covered with planing.

Louise Wagnon was my great-great aunt.

Her sister, Theodosia Wagnon Iles, was my great grandmother. Our family called her, "Doten."

She lived long enough for me to sit beside her rocker on the Old House dogtrot porch, right beside the log sills.

That's where many of my best stories came from.

The Old House precluded the creation of Beauregard Parish in 1913.

Virgin pines don't rot. The sill remains as solid as the day they placed it over one hundred and thirty years ago.

I believe it's here to stay.

🌰

I am a student of symbolism.

Things we can see can symbolize unseen things. That's what the log sill at The House in Dry Creek, Louisiana, means to me.

135 seps from porch to porch.

That's not very far.

Then again, it can't be measured.

The two homes of my family.

Unseen things like family.

Spiritual faith.

Legacy.

Love.

Relationships,

And Memories.

May it ever be so.

"Everyone then who hears these words of mine and does them will be like a wise man who built his house on the rock. And the rain fell, and the floods came, and the winds blew and beat on that house, but it did not fall, because it had been founded on the rock."
—Jesus in Matthew 7:24

NOTES FOR MY FUTURE SELF:

49

END NOTES

"When a book leaves your hands, it belongs to God. He may use it to save a few souls or try a few others, but I think that for the writer to worry is to take over God's business."
—Flannery O'Connor

Lord, here it is. Take and use it.

Reader, this is no longer my book. It belongs to you. Enjoy it, scribble in it, make it your *own* personal copy, then share about it with others.

Remember that a book needs friends before it needs readers. If you enjoy our writing, please help spread the word about *The Three Trees* as well as all of our Creekbank books.

In Appreciation

A well-made and well-written book has so many fingerprints all over it. These are some of my special friends who helped bring *The Three Trees* to life.

Tim Conner, Carolyn Boniol, Kitty Murphy, Kathy Ward, Thelma Boothe, Larry Wise, Matheus Alves,, Deb Tyler, Noah Iles, Jude Iles, Luke Iles, Jack Iles, Sydney Iles, Emma Iles, Maggie Iles, Eliza Iles, Mary Iles, Keirsten LeJuene, Mary Gardner, Angela Donovan, Brenda Brechtel, Quinn Williams, Aaron Hankins, Amanda Phillips, the Happy Baristas at Tamp and Grind Coffee, Wayne Mullins and Lynn Duck, Kitty Murphy, Sharon Dodson, and countless others whose fingerprints are hidden on these pages as well as in my heart.

Most of all, I thank my wife, DeDe. I couldn't do anything, especially write a book, without your encouragement and belief in me. I'm enjoying this season and journey with you. You've always been my favorite traveling partner.

A word to my "Co-Authors:" Thank you for your songs, quotes, poems, and stories that have enriched the pages of *The Three Trees*.

The Three Trees is one of the few books that quote the Lord Jesus Christ, Noah Iles and Jason Isbell, Ann Landers and Woody, Jethro and his son-in-law Moses, Chester Nimitz and Henry Stimson, Warren Morris and Coach Skip Bertman, Willie Nelson and Todd Strain, Sylvester Stallone and Dean Christian, Emmitt Smith and Frederick Douglas, Ed King and Mike King, the Apostle Paul and James, the brother of the Lord Jesus, Don Gray and Henry David Thoreau, The Lone Ranger and Tonto, Molly Anderson and Zig Ziglar, Canned Heat and Donnie Reeves, Robert Sanders and Robert E. Lee, Red Colquitt and the Red Clay Strays, Albert and Lucille Ortis, Mark Twain and C.G. Terry, Kirk Cooper and The Drive By Truckers, Seth Godin and Calvin Coolidge, Debra Tyler and Wendell Berry, Lloyd Iles and Seneca the Younger.

Noah and Curt Iles
Tamp and Grind Coffee Alexandria, Louisiana

About

Noah Iles is a graduating senior at Alexandria (Louisiana) Senior High and plans to attend Louisiana Tech and major in Mechanical Engineering. He is the oldest grandson of Curt and DeDe Iles. Noah created the interior design for *The Three Trees*.

Curt Iles writes from his hometown of Dry Creek, Louisiana. He is the author of fifteen books celebrating the people, culture, and history of Louisiana's Pineywoods.

He and his wife DeDe live in Alexandria, Louisiana, near their nine grandchildren. You can reach Curt at creekbank.stories@gmail.com or through his website at www.creekbank.net.

His books, ebooks, audiobooks, are available at Amazon/Curt Iles/Creekbank Stories, and on Ingram Content.

A final note from the Author: *The Three Trees* is published using Amazon KDP (Kindle Direct Publishing.) this means the author can update the manuscript at will.

Here's where you come in: In spite of extensive editing, there will be typos, misuse of grammar, and minute errors in this book. I've never read a book that didn't have some pesky typo hidden among the pages.

I'd appreciate your feedback on those critters. Let's root them out together. Help me correct *anything* that *distracts* the discerning reader.

Email me at creekbank.stories@gmail.com with the location, pages, paragraph of the error. I only ask that you also include iyour favorite story (and why) in *The Three Trees*. In appreciation, I'll send a heartfelt thank you.

—S.C.I.

Also by Curt Iles

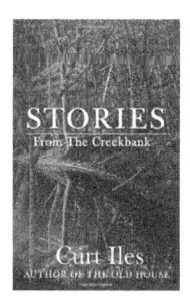

Stories From The Creekbank ISBN 978-0982649251

The Old House   ISBN 1-4033-5227-5

Wind in the Pines   ISBN 978-0-9705236-1-7

Hearts Across the Water   ISBN 978-0-9863026-4-0

Deep Roots   ISBN 978-0-9826492-1-3

The Mockingbird's Song   ISBN   978-0-9705236-9-3

Christmas Jelly   ISBN 978-0-9826492-6-8

The Wayfaring Stranger ISBN978-0-9826492-2-0

A Good Place   ISBN 978-0-9705236-9-3

As The Crow Flies   ISBN 978-0-9705236-7-9

A Spent Bullet   ISBN 978-1-4497-2233-3

Trampled Grass   ISBN 978-0-9863026-9-5

Uncle Sam: A Horse's Tale

Medic ISBN 978-0-9826492-6-8

ISBN 978-0-9863026-0-2 paperback

ISBN 978-1-967796-03-8 hardcover

The Three Trees
Paperback ISBN 978-0--8-8
Ebook ISBN   978-1-967796-02-1
Hardcover ISBN 978-0-9863026
Large Print ISBN 978-1-967796-03-8

All books are available on Amazon and Ingram Distributors.

www.creekbank.net
Email: creekbank.stories@gmail.com
Facebook: TheCreekTribe
Podcast: rss.com/podcasts/thecreek
To learn about speaking opportunities, book clubs, and school visits, email curt@creekbank.net

50

THE TREE

"So many years from now.
Long after we are gone.
This tree will spread its branches out
And bless the dawn."
"Planting Trees"
—Andrew Peterson

Made in the USA
Middletown, DE
27 April 2025

74732801R00170